Speeding up Sport

OXFORD
UNIVERSITY PRESS

Great Clarendon Street, Oxford, ox2 6dp,
United Kingdom

Oxford University Press is a department of the University of Oxford.
It furthers the University's objective of excellence in research, scholarship,
and education by publishing worldwide. Oxford is a registered trade mark of
Oxford University Press in the UK and in certain other countries

© Oxford University Press 2022

The moral rights of the author have been asserted

First Edition published in 2022

Impression: 1

Published in the United States of America by Oxford University Press
198 Madison Avenue, New York, NY 10016, United States of America

British Library Cataloguing in Publication Data

Data available

Library of Congress Control Number: 2022945790

ISBN 978–0–19–286512–0

DOI: 10.1093/oso/9780192865120.001.0001

Printed in India by
Rakmo Press Pvt. Ltd.

Contents

I am very grateful to the professors (Prof. Pranav Desai, Prof. V.V. Krishna, Prof. Saradindu Bhaduri, Prof. Madhav Govind, Prof. Rohan D'Souza) and all the scholars and staff at the Centre for Studies in Science Policy (CSSP), JNU for their support and for always keeping me on my intellectual toes. Thanks are also owed to Prof. Shishir Jha and Prof. Satish Agnihotri at the Centre for Policy Studies (CPS), IIT Bombay for giving me the space—physical, intellectual, financial—to work on this manuscript as a postdoctoral fellow.

A sincere Thank You also to Prof. Mahesh Rangarajan, Prof. Ramachandra Guha, Prof. Shiv Viswanathan, Prof. Prashant Kidambi, and Prof. Aniket Alam for their support over the years, for long and useful conversations, important methodological advice, writing recommendation letters, reading drafts, giving valuable feedback, and for caring about this work. A special thank you to Prof. Ramachandra Guha also for giving this book its name.

I owe another big Thank You to Mr Rajaraman Ganesan, Mrs Rwitticka Kalita, Mr Pravin Amre, Ms Sonam Bajaj, Dr Nalin Mehta, Mr Shane McPherson, and Mr Vikas Chand for all their help during field work.

A very special Thank You to Mr Gideon Haigh, Mr Bishan Singh Bedi, Mr Murali Kartik, Ms Sharda Ugra, Mr Azhar Habib, Mr Hemant Buch, and Mr S. Ramakrishnan for being the most remarkable people that anyone could interview when it comes to cricket.

I could not have survived the PhD and what followed without the support of my colleagues and friends who have fed and watered me (and consequently the thesis) and held me together at so many moments when I could have completely fallen apart. Thank you, Neeladri C, Poonam Pandey, Anshu Ogra, Aarthi Sridhar, Monish Khetrimayum, Marine Al Dahdah, Mathieu Quet, Varun-Vaibhav-Mallika Joshi (and gang!).

A final acknowledgement to the institution of JNU where I spent the years between 2009 and 2016 working on this project, eating at the *dhabas*, marvelling at the nilgai, and learning to be a scholar. JNU has given me (and so many others) the space and opportunity to be able to push the boundaries of academic thought, to understand what it means to be human in this world, to be self-reflexive enough to receive criticism without rancour, and to engage with opposing views without being threatened by them. For that and so much more, thank you.

Introduction

This book is a product of my doctoral research conducted between 2011 and 2016, aimed at initiating a conversation between insights from the field of Science, Technology, and Society (STS) and the sociology and history of cricket in India. The main theme, in its specific thrust, is to explore how information and communication technologies (ICTs) have shaped and determined cricket and the Indian Premier League (IPL) in several ways.

The IPL was set up in 2007 by Lalit Modi as an immediate response to Zee Entertainment Enterprises' Indian Cricket League that was seeking to corner what was perceived as a large market for audiences that wanted to see entertainment collapse into cricket.[1] The League was thus established to be a 'game changer' in the sporting-entertainment arena. It was as much cricket as it was entertainment, peppered liberally as it was with celebrities from cinema, business people, socialites, and cricketers from around the world. Much has been written about the setting up of the IPL,[2,3,4] the auction,[5] and the extravaganza that followed.[6,7] When I submitted my doctoral thesis in 2016, the IPL was eight seasons old, and had had the participation of thirteen teams (including two new teams for the 2016 edition), crowned five winners, awarded several million dollars worth of prize money, and attracted a fair share of controversy and scandal.

My contention is that the IPL in both scale and scope was primarily developed as India's first 'sporting platform' rather than a cricket tournament. And critical to the assembling of the IPL—as a profound and unprecedented rupture in format and design—I suggest, has been the roles, influences, and potentialities created by a range of ICTs. By a sporting platform, I assert that the IPL is more akin to being run in function and form as an assemblage of sorts; there has been a complicated crowding onto a single platform of otherwise disparate interests, elements, and calculations such as big businesses, Bollywood, military technologies,

Speeding up Sport. Vidya Subramanian, Oxford University Press. © Oxford University Press 2022.
DOI: 10.1093/oso/9780192865120.003.0001

The history of cricket is a story of its evolution from being an elite 'gentleman's game' that was only played by the British elite to having become the collective obsession of the people of some of Britain's erstwhile colonies. In his book, *A Corner of a Foreign Field*, Ramachandra Guha writes of the historical linkages between a sport that was introduced by colonial rulers and integrated into the fabric of nation-making and nationalism. So much so, that the pressure on the national cricket team as ambassadors and flag bearers of the country became immense.[13] He has also examined cricket by exploring its implications and impacts for caste, class, and religions in India (for example, the Bombay Quadrangular and Pentangular series in which teams were divided along religious lines). Guha discusses the case of Palwankar Baloo, arguably India's first 'great' player. Even though Baloo was one of the better players in the team (he took more than 100 wickets during the 1911 season in England as part of an all-Indian team), he would be made to sit apart from the rest of the team during breaks because of his low (*Chamaar*) caste. Guha has also written of the deep and intricate relation between politics and cricket in India. Speaking of politics and cricket intertwining not only within the administration of cricket but also in the use of cricket as a unifying national symbol, Guha writes of posters that appeared during the riots of 1984 that featured Kapil Dev, Mohammed Azharuddin, Roger Binny, and Maninder Singh, exhorting people to 'play together, live together'. Subsequent to the 1983 World Cup victory, cricketers had become superstars in their own right, and the Government had tried to use their celebrity as a pacifying influence on the rioting public. Following the development and transformations in cricket, Guha has also written about the changes that the game has seen in going from test matches to one-day games and now to the new Twenty20 form of cricket.[14,15]

In *The Tao of Cricket*, Ashis Nandy views cricket through a cultural lens, and speaks of how 'some arguments of colonial, neo-colonial, anti-colonial, and post-colonial consciousness can be made better in the language of international cricket than of political economy'.[16] He writes of the changes in cricket as it has become a billion-dollar enterprise from being a mainly Victorian sport. And in this process, Nandy contends that it has become 'softer' as a cultural form, and has moved away from its original cultural role as 'a typically nineteenth century game, enshrining pre-industrial values in an industrial society and serving as a critique of the latter'.[17]

Other scholars such as Boria Majumdar have also studied cricket, particularly the intermingling of cricket and politics in the Subcontinent, the effects of commercialization on the game, and the role of television and media. Majumdar has argued that even news channels are dependent on cricket for revenue, citing the example of how the elections of the Cricket Association of Bengal (CAB) dominated the news channels in July 2006. With elements of factional politics (between Jyoti Basu and Buddhadeb Bhattacharya), a whiff of the politics at the centre (Sharad Pawar and his tussle with the Congress party), and the ouster of Bengal's hero Saurav Ganguly from the national team; a local sports body election had become the country's most important news story of the week.[18]

Majumdar has also written about the IPL and its influences on cricket. He has argued that the debate over whether the transformation of cricket into a commercial entity is good or bad is unimportant because in order to survive as a 'global sport', cricket must embrace the path of commercialization. According to Majumdar, the more relevant point of argument is whether such commercialization will eventually 'filter down to the grassroots and herald an overall improvement in the game's health as is being touted or will it, even if inadvertently, weaken the foundation of cricket'.[19]

In many ways, the 'event' of a cricket match today is not just the innings that are played out on the cricket pitch. With the entry of big business, glamour, advertising, and brand management, a lot more rides on cricket than the game alone. Nalin Mehta has written on the subject of the influence of television in Indian cricket as he speaks of the rise of cricket coinciding with the rise of television viewership in India. He extrapolates this theory to include in his analysis the possibility that the rise of cricket in India has not necessarily stemmed 'from some peculiar Indian affiliation for the game, but (is) inextricably linked with the expansion of Indian television and a confluence of other factors: the creation of a large middle class, economic reforms, the politics of identity, the birth of the satellite television industry and broader trends in globalization'.[20] Other analyses of cricket include a scrutiny of the relationship between media and sport. For example, the case of the website *cricinfo.org* which began

such as the medium of television. Adding to the tumult is the extensive use of ICTs, social media, and the internet not just to discuss the match at hand but also to advertise, express opinion (and even help form them), and indulge in other peripheral activities.

The manner in which cricket has been reassembled into a platform has led to the identification of players as 'brands' in themselves. Apart from the obvious celebrity that comes with being a successful sportsperson, there are now the added layers of brand management, public relations, positioning in the media, and the monetary 'value' of a player as seen through endorsements, etc.

In recent years, there has been a growing scholarship trying to link sports and social phenomenon, and academics are beginning to theorize this relation. Studies, such as that by Günther Lüschen,[24] provide a broad framework to show how sport, originally an institution of social behaviour that possessed at its core a sense of competition that is based on skill and strategy, has today grown to extend into education, economics, and even mass media. I have tried to view the phenomena of sport (particularly cricket) through the lens of STS to gain an understanding of the relationship of cricket with technology, and chart the course that it took in becoming not just a popular sport but also a platform and a vessel for the promotion of several new constituencies.

I believe that one is better able to grasp the transformations in cricket through the years when they are seen as a series of contingent twists and turns, and not as a straightforward path. The story of cricket is marked with instances of great turmoil that have shaken the cricketing establishment to its core—be it Douglas Jardine's Bodyline series, Kerry Packer's World Series Cricket, the betting scandal that implicated Hansie Cronje, or the more recent birth of the IPL and its attending scandals. It is possible to view the major changes in the transformation of the game—from five-day test matches to one-day cricket to Twenty20—as a series of ruptures in the traditional fabric of the game.

It is my intention to use STS as a backdrop to understand the game of cricket and its changing relationship with technology. Technology has not just played a role in the way that sport reaches its audience but also the way it is played. In cricket, practically every aspect of the game has witnessed enormous changes propelled by technological change: umpiring, coaching, broadcasting, and of course, playing the game itself. These changes have led to further transformations in the way that cricket is accessed, understood, discussed, and administrated.

Studying Up

I have attempted to focus on the specific contexts in which certain events have unfolded in order to understand the historical and cultural settings of the subject. I have drawn upon the anthropological concept of 'Studying Up' to theorize and better understand the problem at hand. Alongside STS, this approach also touches upon certain aspects of media and cultural studies in order to sociologically grasp the varied connections between the realm of sport, media, celebrity, and spectatorship.

Laura Nader, in her paper, *Up the Anthropologist: Perspectives Gained from Studying Up*, establishes the importance for anthropologists to study the middle and upper end of the social power structure, as well as the lower.[25] She postulates that 'studying up' as well as down would lead one to ask many 'common sense' questions in reverse. She also suggests that the consequences of not studying up could be serious in terms of developing adequate theory and description. An important question on power relations between the researcher and the researched is asked. She asks, 'What if, in reinventing anthropology, anthropologists were to study the colonisers rather than the colonised, the culture of power rather than the culture of powerlessness, the culture of affluence rather than the culture of poverty?'

It is as important, Nader posits, to study the rich and powerful, as it is to study the poor and the downtrodden. An ethnographic study of the upper echelons of society would be of great use in understanding not just those strata but their relationships and power equations that then shape and percolate down to the rest of society. Instead of looking at people from so-called 'elite' parts of society—one that perhaps I myself belong to—as living within an impenetrable wall of their own 'elite-ness'; such a methodology would allow one to make that way of life more accessible and be as much under scrutiny as, perhaps, a distant tribe in a far off land.[26]

Nader recognizes the problems in such an approach and lists the main obstacles that prevent more such anthropological study in terms of 'access, attitudes, ethics and methodology'. The powerful are often out of reach, and the problems of objectivity can become important when conducting research within one's own society. In the case of this study, several participants in Focus Group Discussions were members of a similar social stratum as I. A few of them objected to my using their discussion as a field study. One participant left a discussion after expressing an opinion that she felt like a 'lab rat'. But at other times, the familiarity worked in my favour since the participants were comfortable expressing their opinions freely in my presence.

I believe that my work falls under the purview of 'studying up' since the people who are the subjects of the research—cricket players, coaches, business people, television personalities, commentators, software engineers, and even the spectators—are all people who can be classified as belonging to a certain 'elite' section of the society in which we live. Apart from the fundamental problem of accessibility (it has proven to be very hard to reach several of the individuals who I wished to interview, and in fact, quite impossible in many cases), there is also the problem of secrecy and celebrity that I have had to face.

Several people who I interviewed have been unwilling to share certain opinions and information that they believe may adversely affect their careers. Opinions that they might express in private could not be expressed on record, and indeed some of them were contract-bound to preserve the secrecy of their companies, teams, and other institutions. A lot of the information gleaned from such interviews could not directly be attributed to the individuals in question due to these quandaries of secrecy and anonymity.

A Quick Word on What's Missing

This research effort has been an exploration of technological influx into the sport in general and cricket in particular. The birth of the IPL, aided as it has been by ICTs, has led to several events that I have not been able to explore in the scope of this effort. One of the big elephants in the room of cricket in the contemporary world is that of corruption. This work has not touched upon the big controversies of match-fixing and corruption that have shaken the cricketing edifice to its core in more than one instance. While I did come across several references to corruption and the techno-logical mediations in it, the scope and scale of including this topic would have taken another entire thesis effort. While I remain deeply interested in the phenomenon, and much can be written about the technological influences that enable and allow such fixing, etc., it remains beyond the scope of this research effort.

* * *

This book is divided into five major chapters. The first is an engagement with the era of test matches, before the limited-overs game came to be and deals with the evolution of the five-day test match into the one-day game. It attempts to describe the game in a pre-television era, in which the result of a match was not what happened at the end, but the process of getting to the end. The game was constructed in the minds of the fans and spectators through a plural narrative, gradually, in several layers, through several media, constructed through many steps, often much after the game had ended.

The shift to a limited-overs game came to be because of the finan-cial crisis faced by cricket in England. As revenues from gate money, etc. for matches dwindled, and the so-called 'Golden Age' of cricket was behind them, English administrators came up with the idea of a limited-overs game to save the finances of clubs and regional sides. Once corporate sponsors entered the fray, the game had truly changed. Next step: technology.

The second chapter deals with the understanding and evolution of technology within the sport of cricket. In a technologically unmediated age of cricket, it was a game played only in the test match, five-day format. With the advent of television and other forms of engagement with the game, not only have two new formats of the game arisen but also a continuous influx of technological mediation has occurred; be it in the dressing room in terms of training and preparation or in the realm of umpiring such as the third umpire and the Decision Review System.

Technological aids such as videographing are now extensively used to shape and mould a cricketer and coaching up and coming cricketers has become an industry in itself. With coaching remotely becoming an option, some players are even opting for individual coaches that are independent of the coaches of the team they play for.[27] Such coaches don't even need to travel with the players. They are able to see their bowling or batting action through the videos recorded during match play and then provide advice and technical expertise over the internet or the phone. This is not to say that the physical presence of the coach has been entirely done away with, but in cases where a personal coach is unable to travel with the player, ICTs allow for such remote coaching to become a reality.

Thus ICTs have become the backbone not just of broadcast technology but also of coaching and player management. Research is being conducted and simulation technologies for dealing with various pitches, bowlers, etc., are being constantly created and modified by software engineers around the globe. From a better 3-D analysis of videotaped bowling action to safer padding for elbow guards, technology has infiltrated every aspect of the game—both on the field and off it.

The third chapter focuses on broadcast technologies of television and the manner in which it has changed/influenced the sport, the sportsperson, and the spectator. There is no sport without television. Even the Olympics are only considered a success when the event is held in a time zone that is friendly to western television audiences.[28] This can be taken to mean that unless there are enough people to watch an event (and the advertisements of the businesses that fund the event), the event has not been a success. This makes television and the internet very potent tools in the hands of marketing professionals, who use events with large public followings such as Wimbledon or the FIFA World Cup as vehicles for promotion.

Even as televised sport provides a great channel for marketing, it provides an enormous opportunity for individual celebrity. Close-ups of individuals and the ability to transform every moment into a dramatic slow-motion replay make television a potent tool for a celebrity to cash in on their own fame, and indeed to create it. The promotion, management, and positioning of the brand of a sportsperson have spawned an entire industry of sports management, thus proving the importance of sport to business and of business to sport.

Televised sport is no longer just watched on the television set. With the growing use of second screen (laptops and computers) and third screen (mobile phones) devices, 'networked media sport'[29] has become the buzzword. It is important to note here that while the screens may be different, the content being broadcast on any screen is almost identical. The feeds for online viewing are usually exactly the same as the ones broadcast live on television. Thus the fear that online Internet Protocol Television (IPTV) might displace the traditional viewing of sport on television has proved unfounded. There are a few extra add-ons in online viewing such as extra camera angles and the ability to share snippets on social media and comment on forums, but the viewing experience can still be counted as a television experience.

The fourth chapter attempts to analyse the spectator and understand the question of who watches, why, and how. The spectator is at the centre of the show that television puts on. The entire edifice of networked media sport and the sporting-entertainment complex is premised on the understanding that sport is popular; and that millions of people around the world watch sport and therefore provide an easy catchment area for those seeking to be seen. The spectator—in the stadium, on television, on mobile phone screens, in public spaces—is at the centre of all spectacle. The behaviour of this spectator is then of paramount importance.

While the first ring of spectators of a sporting event exists within the stadium in which it is taking place, the main 'audience' of a sporting event is, curiously, absent from the site of the spectacle. The watching 'crowd' now exists in what Paul Virilio has called the 'city of the instant'[30] and encompasses the entire group of people around the world who are 'watching' the event on screens everywhere—at home on TVs, on mobile phones, computers, laptops, and tablets. This displaced, non-homogeneous 'crowd' is the main target of the platform that sport is. 'Those absent from the stadium are always right', posits Virilio, as he points to those whose wishes seemingly dictate how a sporting event is 'produced'.[31]

It would be impossible to construct this edifice without the substratum of ICTs. The bringing together of large groups of fans online on social media, the near-continuous engagement of sport and television anchors with content generated by users and fans (such as tweets and Facebook posts), and even the marketing and advertising gimmicks that lure audiences are necessarily mediated by ICTs. Understanding this complicated moment in which a cricket fan is constructed both as a spectator and as a consumer is aided by looking at the entire IPL sporting-entertainment complex through the lens of Paul Virilio's idea of the politics of speed.

The fifth chapter deals with theories of society and technology in order to understand the manner in which and reasons for the game to have evolved in the way that it has. In writing about the ever-narrowing margins of Olympic records, Paul Virilio makes the observation that the better the sportspersons performed, the smaller became the advances they made, so much so that 'they could only be noticed electronically'.[32] He wonders what will happen as these margins become even smaller. 'One day, the champion will disappear in the limits of his own record', he writes. The basic argument that Virilio makes about speed is that as speed continues to increase, it creates a disconnect with the space on which it is created. In its simplest terms, speed makes it possible to reduce the amount of time it takes to travel from one place to the other—be it in vehicles that transport people or electronic signals that relay sound and images to television sets, or data transfer across the internet that allow voice messages and video conversations. For Virilio, each of these dromological states necessarily creates a 'negation of space itself'.[33]

Virilio then goes on to suggest that engaging in the continuous displays that television bombards us with creates in the viewer or spectator a condition of 'picnolepsy'. He describes this condition as one in which 'a subject undergoes momentary lapses of memory and must continually reconstruct a narrative based on the fragmentary evidence that remains'. Dependence on such technologies causes the spectator, Virilio argues, to become disconnected from the lived reality of his or her own life.

Televised entertainment, and consequently sport, are subject to the same criticism. Instead of playing the sport—in the sweat and mud real-world—spectators of sport watch it on sanitized, unidimensional screens, thus disconnecting the spectator from the guts and blood drama that the sport actually is. Even the sweat dripping off a player's brow is caught in slow motion and depicted as an image on the televised broadcast. The cold and rain in a football match, the wind speed interfering with a tennis shot or the mosquitoes on a subcontinent cricket field become background embellishments only heard of if the commentators—mediators between the audience and the sport—choose to comment upon them.

As cricket, and indeed all sport, becomes mediated through technologies of entertainment and communication, they have become commodities that fit right into the consumerist society we live in. Zygmunt Bauman, writing of the 'liquid modern' world we inhabit today, describes the modern-day citizen simultaneously as both a consumer and a commodity. Bauman argues that everything in the liquid modern world is commodifiable.[34]

It is for and from this flighty, 'nowist'[35] society that the sporting-entertainment complex has been constructed as a platform. It provides the corporate sponsors and their advertisers a place from which to be seen by a massive number of potential consumers. It also provides movie stars and socialites another platform to be seen by their adoring fans; and the sport a new version to appeal to a new generation of sport fans, whose attentions are being vied for by several other sports and entertainment options. Facilitated at every step by ICTs, the IPL as a new version of the sport is more than a sport, more than just cricket, and more than simply an advertising platform.

1

'A Dramatic Spectacle'

Cricket before Technology

As a sport, cricket has always had an appeal that was different from other mainstream sports. Consider cricket when the only form played at the highest level was the test match: a slow and deliberately paced affair, with breaks every few overs. Drinks breaks every hour, a break for lunch, and one for tea, and a single match going on for the better part of a week. There is hardly any other sport that requires the sort of commitment from fans that cricket does. One match took five (sometimes six) entire days to complete, often resulting in no result at all—a draw. And yet, it has proved to be satisfying for all parties concerned—the two playing teams and the spectators too (Ramachandra Guha even called the draw 'central to the magic and mystique of cricket'[1]). Ashis Nandy makes the point that in cricket, victory and defeat are not the clear terms that they are in most other sports. In this game, while victory was judged to be better than a draw and a drawn game certainly better than defeat, it was seen as more honourable to lose grandly than to win ingloriously or succumb to a 'tame' draw.[2]

The result of the game was not a single point in time. It was a process. Much like a good play or a movie, the meaning of a cricket match was not so much in the climax, as it was in everything else that happened in the middle. C.L.R. James calls cricket 'first and foremost a dramatic spectacle' that he compares not with other sports but with theatre, ballet, opera, and even dance.[3] James concedes that a kind of drama is at the centre of most sports; and the trials of the two sides engaged in a boxing match or a running race too 'exhibit skill, courage, endurance and sharp changes of fortune; can evoke hope and fear, harrow the soul with laughter and tears, pity and terror'. But, he argues, cricket is far more a dramatic spectacle than most sports. He makes the point that at the heart of cricket is a very

Speeding up Sport. Vidya Subramanian, Oxford University Press. © Oxford University Press 2022.
DOI: 10.1093/oso/9780192865120.003.0002

fundamental conflict between two individuals that is 'strictly personal but no less strictly representative of a social group'.

James expands the analogy of the dramatic spectacle by describing how dramatists and novelists strive to give individual characters in plays and novels that deeper engagement with the larger narrative of the play or story; for that point on stage when a character becomes himself and a representative of a bigger whole at the same time. Similarly, in sports such as football and even relay running, individual players may find themselves becoming the sole representative of their side at certain moments during the course of play. But in cricket, he argues, the two individuals engaged in combat—the batsman at the crease and the bowler for the particular over—in the time span of every single ball being bowled, are not merely representatives of the two playing sides, but become, in that instant, the sides themselves. They thus elaborately play out, unlike in most other games, the complex relationship between the individual and the social. According to James, 'What other sports, games, and arts have to aim at, the players (in cricket) are given to start with, they cannot depart from it'. He goes on to say, 'This fundamental relation of the One and the Many, Individual and Universal, leader and followers, representative and ranks, the part and the whole, is structurally imposed on the players of cricket'.

Cricket was a slow sport. The five-day test match, unlike the newer versions of the game, gave a batsman the chance to pace his innings—to, in cricketing parlance, 'get his eye in' (in cricket at that time, it was almost always a 'he'). To begin with, it was okay to spend an over or two testing the pitch, getting used to the conditions, and understanding the strategies of the other side. It worked for the fielding side equally well. They could take a few overs to understand the psyche of the batsman on that particular day, in that particular innings. The game, as so many practitioners of cricket have claimed, was played in the minds of the players.

The slowness of the game, which has often been blamed for declining viewer interest in test cricket in recent times, was part of the allure of cricket. It was a game shorn of the idea of speed. While fast-paced, edge-of-the-seat action was certainly part of the package, it was not constantly and continuously played at high-adrenaline levels. The speed, or lack thereof, in the play itself appeared to give the players more opportunity for guile, for thought, for strategy. In a five-day match with two innings each, a player has an opportunity to pace his innings; and indeed to employ a skill that requires patience, strategy, speed, and endurance in equal quantities. It was a game involving as much the strength of the mind, as it did the skills of batting, bowling, and fielding.

A bowler, even if bowling well, could be proving expensive if a batsman in form is able to read his bowling well on that particular day. When his tricks seem not to be working, he is pulled off and rested and brought on for a spell later on or from the other end. The batsman, when confronted with an in-form bowler, may adopt a similar tactic. Lie low while the in-form bowler bowls, and attack another one. The sum of the parts of a good test match always seemed greater than the whole. The result, in some ways, was incidental. It was possible, as Nandy has pointed out, to lose graciously. It was also possible for a team's victory to pale in comparison to an excellent performance on the field—a double century or excellent bowling figures, for instance. The end result of the match, as C.L.R. James points out, was not of great importance. 'Appreciation of cricket', as he put it, 'has little to do with the end'.

A cricket match did not necessarily lead to the *event* of the result. It was brought to a fitting conclusion through thought, experiment, and strategy. It arrived at its climax via—invoking the dramatic metaphor once again—grand soliloquies, quiet solid background pieces, blistering action hero stuff, life-altering moments, the odd cameo performances, and even small and imperative subplots.

A Plural Narrative

Cricket was always a spectator sport. It has always been the crowds at stadia—for everything from the Bombay Pentangular series in pre-independence India to county cricket in England to international fixtures around the world—that have kept the game alive. In 1972–73, when the English team visited India, the crowds in stadia were so large (writing in *The Illustrated Weekly*, Raju Bharatan pointed out that the number of people at Eden Gardens in Calcutta may have been almost twice the number of available seats) that several visiting players felt that they were at a disadvantage because the crowd was so vociferously behind the Indian players. Bharatan's pointing out that the partisan nature of the crowd should not bother the visitors because the money brought in by these crowds does not;[4] is a reminder that the fuel on which a sport may become successful must be the audience for it.

And cricket has always had its audience. Reading C.L.R. James' book *Beyond a Boundary* gives one a fair idea of the kind of following that the game has had in West Indies, in Australia, and in England. James brings out the palpable excitement in the common people for everything cricket—from Saturday afternoon fixtures of the Lancashire League in England and club cricket in the West Indies to international fixtures at Lord's in London or at the Queen's Park Oval in Trinidad.

This was an age before television replays and large screens in stadia. To be able to see (and more importantly, feel and understand) the brilliance of a shot, the spectator would have had to either watch very closely from the stands every stroke a batsman played and every ball a bowler bowled, or wait for a radio commentator to describe it or some newspaper reporter to *write the image* in the thousand words it may have taken, to be read the day after the match. Cricket writer Gideon Haigh spoke to me[5] about how 'unusual' cricket was among games, in that 'the action takes place far away from the spectator and the interpreter, and there's a big distance to bridge; and that distance actually opens up scope for imagination'. Echoing James, he described the process of writing up cricket 'in a sense is almost like a piece of theatre criticism, or a piece of literary criticism'.

The game of cricket with the white flannel contrasting against the green grass of the cricket field and with its 'dramatic spectacle' in every ball is highly suitable for visual consumption. The run-up of a bowler like the 6 feet, 7 inches tall Tony Greig with his hair flying behind him, striking terror in the hearts of batsmen, must have been a sight to behold. As also the perfect stance and action of a straight drive over the bowler's head from the bat of someone like Don Bradman. And yet, while these greats played, the visual was not the primary form of the narrative of cricket. While it was embedded in the narrative and was the ultimate end achieved through radio and writing, it had to be constructed, individually, in the mind of every spectator, not consumed directly.

A breakthrough in visual technology for cricket came on 24 June 1938. It was the first day of the second test of the Ashes at Lord's Cricket Ground. History was made at 11.29 a.m., as Ernie McCormick of Australia bowled the opening over to Charlie Barnett of England. For the first time ever, a cricket match was seen by audiences outside the stadium. It was the first time ever that a cricket match was telecast live on TV by the BBC,[6] and the legendary Teddy Wakelam became the first television commentator for cricket. With only three cameras and no-frills, it was a far cry from the blitzkrieg that televised cricket is today, but a beginning had been made. Perhaps it would not be too far-fetched to conjecture that cricket as we know it today began its evolution on that day. But it would still be several decades before televised cricket changed the face of the game. At this time in 1938, cricket was still very much a sport of the five-day test match. And innovations to television broadcasts such as the slow-motion replay and even something that we take completely for granted today, such as cameras at both bowling ends, were quite a long way in the future. Television sets were not yet a ubiquitous presence in homes, and radio commentary too was in its infancy. This form of relaying cricket matches, of course, would turn out to be far more successful in the years to come, becoming the primary way for people outside stadia to keep track of matches till as recently as the early 1980s.

It was commentators such as Teddy Wakelam who brought the match alive for listeners outside the stadium. Wakelam was a pioneer in the field of radio commentary. He is credited with a number of firsts, not least of which was him being at the helm of the first-ever blow-by-blow broadcast of any sporting clash—in January 1927, he commentated on the England v Wales cricket match at Twickenham. An expert at a number of sports, one of the more famous stories about him is at Wimbledon in the mid-1930s, where during one live broadcast, he accidentally set fire to his papers, and yet continued speaking unruffled as though nothing of import had transpired. Without scorers or summarizers to help, Wakelam was of a breed of commentators that held their own in a match and would have been a pleasure to listen to even if it was not cricket they were talking about.

Radio commentary for cricket actually began in 1922, but it was more in the way of reporting the match than ball-by-ball commentary. A few years later, in the 1930s, 'synthetic' broadcasts began to fill the gap that arose when the BBC would only report innings scores. According to Christian Ryan for *Crininfo* magazine, 'Stepping into the breach, French radio station *Poste Parisien* hired former Australian all-rounder Alan Fairfax, put him in a Paris studio, fed him detailed reports of play by cable and had him report the game in the present tense as if he were actually watching.[7]

Synthetic radio would go a step further before ball-by-ball coverage became commonplace. In June 1938 in Australia, a rudimentary written description of play was cabled in from England after every over and the four commentators in the studio—Alan McGilvray, Vic Richardson, Monty Noble, and Hal Hooker—would transform the information into a riveting ball-by-ball commentary. According to Ryan, 'a pencil striking wood replicated the thwack of leather on willow; a gramophone recreated the cheers and jeers of a faraway crowd. Bradman-obsessed Australians listened all night long'.

It was not long before a shift to running commentary took shape, and it soon became the chief medium of audience engagement with the sport of cricket. The visual constructed through thickly descriptive reporting and voice modulated audio commentary became the order of the day. Listeners were kept in raptures as the breathless frenzy of radio commentary described every shot—beginning with the run-up of the bowler, describing the pitching and turning of the ball, going on to describe in accurate detail the batsman's response, his stroke, the placement of the ball, the response of the fielder—the commentator's voice rising with excitement for a catch or a chase to the boundary—and the return throw—ripe with the possibility of a runout, an overthrow, or a stopped single—to get the ball back to the wicket-keeper or bowler; and then it would begin again.

The listener, in their mind's eye, was transported to the stadium. In fact, several people in the stands would have radios with them to get a better idea of what was happening on the field. It was a common sight to see groups of people in street corners and shops huddled around a single transistor listening intently—their faces ripe with a tension that reflected the emotion in the commentator's voice—as they followed an ongoing match.

The other important medium through which audiences engaged with cricket was that of the written word. Detailed match reports and scorecards, accompanied by news from off the field, and often an image or two were indispensable for newspapers the day after an important match. These reports gave fans a detailed account of all that had transpired, both on and off the field. Newspaper reporting in that time when television was not as omnipresent as today involved a writing style that was far more graphic and detailed. Since the readers had not already heard expert analyses and detailed discussions by the time they read the newspapers, the description of the game was far more meticulous and nuanced, aimed at giving the reader a comprehensive view of the match. For instance, describing India's incredible 59-run victory against Australia in Melbourne in 1981, R. Mohan of *The Hindu* wrote,

> (Kim) Hughes was the batsman with the best temperament and the strokes against spin on a turning wicket, but he let his side down by attempting to cut (Dilip) Doshi off the stumps and the ball that straightened up and came quickly off the pitch crashed into the bottom of his off stump ... The base of the stump took quite a few knocks today from Kapil Dev. The cheeky left-hander (Rod) Marsh was an important batting figure in such a crisis and Kapil Dev got rid of him quickly with a leg-cutter having him play down the wrong line, in a glide shot.[8]

The closest a fan got to actually *seeing* the game without being present in the stadium was through associated photographs in newspapers and magazines (although some might argue that this kind of *seeing* was better in quality than what one *saw* from the stands in the stadium). Accompanying the article cited above was an image of Kapil Dev in action, not in the match being discussed, but adequate for the purpose of visualization. The image showed to full merit the graceful bowling action for which 'The Haryana Hurricane' was famous.

The first real glimpse, so to speak, of actually imagining the spectacle on the field for the spectator outside the stadium came from radio commentary. But live, running commentary tends, naturally, to be fast-paced, having to move from ball to ball, incident to incident as it was occurring on the field. Even at times when the pace of the game was slow, commentators kept listeners in thrall by sharing interesting titbits such as statistics of players, venue information, and other trivia. But while listening to the live-running commentary, there was hardly the time to build the image of the match in one's head, complete with details of strokeplay and bowling action. This sort of construction required a slower and far more descriptive means—that of the written word, which came the next day in newspapers. While not every stroke and action can be described in a newspaper article, the written word managed to construct images that can perhaps rival actually seeing it happen in front of one's own eyes. The point is illustrated by a description by C.L.R. James. He describes a shot once played by Wilton St. Hill that was not one of his usual grace and elegance shots. 'There was a primitive hidden in him', writes James recounting what St. Hill would do if a bowler blocked his leg-glance, and then goes on to describe the shot:

> He stretched his left foot down the wicket and, with a sweep that seemed to begin from first-slip and encompassed the whole horizon, smashed the ball hard and low to square-leg. Sweep is not the correct word. It was a swing, begun when the ball was almost within reach, and carried out with a violence that seemed aimed at the ball personally, to hit it out of sight or break it to bits.[9]

The point of note here is that the description of the game, whether or not accompanied by an illustrative image or two, appeared *after* the match was over. And several times, as was seen above, the image accompanying a newspaper or magazine article was not even from the match in question. Also, the report did not necessarily bring to the reader any brand new information that they did not previously know. In fact, most often, the interested reader was almost always aware of the sequence of events and the main highlights of the match by the time the report was read; and yet these articles were immensely popular and looked forward to.

It almost seems as if the memory of the match lingered longer when no one could see it happening, than today, when every shot and every skirmish is seen and can be replayed as many times as one wishes. Replaying the main events of the match through newspaper reports brought attention to those details that embellish the visual in the spectator's mind that has already been painted by the commentary during the match.

There seemed to be no need (yet) to make the spectacle of test cricket more spectacular in order to engage its audience. The pace of the game itself was slow, and so it seemed not to bother audiences that the visual of the match was constructed slowly—in bits—by audio commentary, match reports, and individual imagination. As the image of the match became sharper and more embellished with greater details and more description, a match could stay in the memory of its audience for much longer, as a lasting memory. Ashis Nandy, in *The Tao of Cricket* quotes Neville Cardus, 'Above all, the slowness of cricket, the absence of hurly burly ... allows character to reveal itself... (In cricket we) remember not the scores and the results in after years; it is the men who remain in our minds, in our imagination'.[10]

'There is a secret bond between slowness and memory, between speed and forgetting', says Milan Kundera in his novel *Slowness*. Illustrating the point, he considers a man walking down a road, and suddenly, he wishes to recall something but cannot remember it instantly. Kundera observes that in order to try and remember, the man automatically slows down. Contrast with someone who wishes to forget something disagreeable that he has just been through. This man would subconsciously speed up, 'as if he were trying to distance himself from a thing too close to him in time'. Kundera concludes, 'The degree of slowness is directly proportional to the intensity of memory; the degree of speed is directly proportional to the intensity of forgetting'.[11] Elsewhere in the book, Kundera mourns the loss of the pleasure that accompanies slowness and laments the loss of the 'amblers of yesteryear'.[12] A match by virtue of staying in the memory of spectators for longer, seemed to make a more lasting impact. The era of (technologically unmediated) test cricket was an era of memory, where the pace of the game and the end result were less important than the actual playing out of the match, and matches were remembered as much for their performances as their results. It was a time when the process of reaching a conclusion seemed to matter more than the event of the climax.

The narrative that constructed the visual was a combination of several means of description—radio commentary, the written word, and sometimes, even a stadium experience. This sort of cricket thrived on a plural narrative and was almost as dependent on the art of storytelling as it was on radio's running commentary. All these elements put together—storytelling, radio commentary, the written description, and stadium outings—all came together to constitute the sport itself in some ways. The way a spectator saw individual matches, and consequently the sport as a whole in that era, was very different from today.

By arguing that the format of the five-day test match was becoming less exciting due to the lack of speed and a definite result, cricket administrators were taking the first steps towards creating a kind of cricket that was constructed around the event of the result. It constitutes a break from the plural narratives that constructed the visual of cricket in a way that the *event* of the climax was not the most important part of the story; but was one of the many things that made up the spectacle of cricket.

In the shift from test matches to limited-overs matches, the conclusion seemed to take on a far more significant role than the performances, strategies, actions, and deliberations within the match, almost making the point that the end is more important than the means. In its technologically unmediated form, the sport of cricket was constructed by the interplay of several aspects within the framework of the game that did not necessarily have a direct bearing on the result. In limiting the number of overs in a match of cricket in order to force a result in a shorter span of time, it seems as though the reach and ideas of a unique sport may also have been limited.

Changing the Game

In the 1950s and 60s, cricket in England was facing a financial crisis. Stadium audiences for county matches were dwindling.*[13] This meant a severe loss in revenue for clubs that were heavily dependent on gate money. Many have attributed this to be the chief reason for the introduction of limited-overs or 'knock-out' competitions in cricket. But it is possible to conjecture that the cause for this loss of spectator interest in cricket could be attributed to another slow and almost imperceptible change within the game. The game was plagued with a debilitating case of what C.L.R. James calls 'security'.[14] It is possible that the way that cricketers of the 50s and 60s were playing may have been the reason that brought things to a head and changed the way that the world understood, played, and viewed cricket. Contrasting this to the magnificence of play in the 'Golden Age' (the age of cricketers like C.B. Fry, Ranjitsinghji, and Frank Woolley—according to James, from about 1890 to the start of the First World War), he writes,

---

* According to Memon, the number of spectators at county championship games had reduced from 2,000,000 in 1950 to 700,000 in 1963, and by 1966, the number fell by another 200,000.

If the glory of the Golden Age is to be found in the specific mental attitudes of the men who made it what it was, the drabness of the prevailing style of play should be sought in the same place. The prevailing attitude of the players of 1890–1914 was daring, adventure, creation. The prevailing attitude of 1957 can be summed up in one word—security. The long forward-defensive push, the negative bowling, are the techniques of specialised performers (professional or amateur) in a security-minded age.

At the end of the 1951 season in England, the Marylebone Cricket Club (MCC) announced a sharp increase in the number of matches drawn—fifty per cent as compared to twenty-five per cent in 1938, 1939, 1946, and 1947.[15] Players had begun using ultra-defensive tactics in desperate attempts to stave off defeat, including everything from sledging (a novelty at the time) to painfully slow over rates. Journalist and writer Ayaz Memon has described this time as 'the period of the growth and rise of the professional with his insidious approach that encompassed everything from slow over rates, to sledging to leaving the field for a rub down on the sly ...' While most of such tactics do not raise eyebrows in the present day (or even in the early 1990s when Memon writes, as he readily agrees); but in the fifties, these were tactics that 'asphyxiated' a sport known as 'the gentleman's game'. It thus seems plausible to speculate that it was this sort of behaviour on the field over a period of time that resulted in decreased enthusiasm from English spectators, which in turn directly resulted in decreased attendance at matches, reduced collections at stadia, and triggered a financial crisis at the club level. Limited overs cricket, was created in such an environment after much deliberation in England in order to bring crowds back into stadia and save the dwindling finances of several regional sides.

However, the ills that plagued English cricket were a problem specific to England and were not a worldwide trend. In India and the West Indies, for instance, cricket was a booming success, and with the induction of Pakistan into what was then the Imperial Cricket Conference, more and more new and enthusiastic audiences were being created. But in spite of its success abroad, at what was then the heart of world cricket—England—the malaise was getting worse.

It was also around this time that two new and major technological attractions began to vie for people's attention—the motor car and the television. Memon calls these 'two (of the) most powerful counter-attractions to all established forms of entertainment'. Due to the direness of the situation in its homeland, and the increasing availability of other forms of leisure activities for traditional spectators of cricket, the administrators of the game faced the problem of either revamping the very structure of cricket to bring these audiences back, or face an imminent collapse of the edifice of cricket in England. Thus, in 1963, cricket administrators took the revolutionary step of organizing a tournament of limited-overs, which would involve each side playing one innings and the entire match was to be played within the space of a single day. Not just in restricting the number of overs bowled and in the number of innings played; this step would also see the entry into cricket of what is now its lifeblood: corporate sponsorship. Gordon Ross, in the *Wisden Cricketers' Almanack* of 1974, writes,

> Cricket was prepared to enter into a marriage with commerce in the form of sponsorship. The new competition was called: 'The First-Class Counties Knock-out competition for The Gillette Cup.' In its second year of operating it became simply 'The Gillette Cup'. This marked the beginning of an era when cricket turned the corner from declining gates and multifarious financial problems, to happier times of buoyant balance sheets ... The surgeons who had attended an ailing patient in 1962 had effected a miraculous cure of the financial disease, but in doing so they radically changed the appearance of the patient. In a letter to the Secretary of MCC, dated August 29, 1962, Mr. H.C.L. Garnett, then Managing Director of Gillette, wrote: 'Clearly you are embarking on a major experiment of vital importance not only to the immediate finances but also to the whole future form of first-class cricket. It will call for a new approach to the game by players, public and press alike.' These were, indeed, prophetic words.[16]

This 'marriage with commerce' would prove to be the revitalization of league cricket and was about to explode upon the international stage in a way that nobody could have foreseen. In England, the Gillette Cup would soon make way for several other limited-overs fixtures, itself transforming into the Natwest Trophy as sponsors changed. Even though these matches were not considered 'first class', the tournaments (the John Player Sunday League in 1969, the Benson and Hedges Cup in 1972) became immensely popular. The success of an older Sunday League prompted the BBC to devote four hours every Sunday afternoon to the League. Because of this, according to Memon, 'millions became TV addicts' and it eventually made way for the John Players Sunday League. Within a decade, it was clear that cricket had changed forever when, for the Benson and Hedges Cup, English cricket received a stimulus of £130,000. But this popularity for the new format existed only in England. It was not until the 1975 Prudential World Cup that limited-overs cricket really gained a foothold in the rest of the cricket-playing world (In India, as Memon points out, it would still take longer—till the 1981–82 season—for one-day games to be played seriously).

One of the most telling instances of the disdain with which one-day cricket was treated by the pundits of the game is the refusal of the *Wisden Cricketers' Almanack* to cover the first-ever one-day international match between England and Australia. The 40-over game on 5 January 1971 was hastily arranged after the third test of the 1970–71 Ashes series, at Melbourne, was washed out. As a short-term measure to give the public something to watch, it was agreed to play a day-long match on what would have been the fifth day of the test. England made 190 in 39.4 of their allotted 40 8-ball overs, and Australia won easily with 42 balls to spare. Martin Williamson quotes Australian spinner, Ashley Mallett, as saying after the match, 'They called it the first one-day international which rather surprised me years later ... I thought, "Gee its part of history". That game we thought was a bit of a joke'. But as 40,000 people watched and the media hailing it as an 'overwhelming success',[17] there was enough indication that this new form of cricket may yet prove the pundits wrong.

There is no denying that even then, one-day cricket was an entirely different game from test cricket, resembling it only in outward appearances and, as Richie Benaud pointed out, the fact that the same people played it. By 1978, however, the break with test cricket would go much deeper and a new form of this entirely different game would have exploded on to the imagination of the cricketing world. This sea change can arguably be attributed to one single man who created cricket's biggest crisis since Douglas Jardine's bodyline—Kerry Packer. Packer came to traditional cricket with revolutionary new ideas and rewrote it into a whole new game. The limited-overs game and the influx of corporate money into cricket allowed it to turn into something that became closer to every other sport and less and less like the traditional test match game that had been known as cricket all this while. It was Packer's World Series Cricket (WSC) between 1977 and 1979 that gave us everything from cameras at both ends of the pitch to players wearing coloured clothing and television programming centred around cricket to making individual players into brands (more on Packer and the WSC in Chapter 3).

A New Turn

The changes that came into cricket were not merely cosmetic. The game itself had been altered. Apart from new camera angles, stump mikes, and coloured clothing, a basic element of cricket had been altered—the result was no longer a sidelight to the game. It became the primary aim. For the batting side, scoring runs became the only aim, no matter how they came. Many connoisseurs of the game lamented the loss of batting technique and style because of this need. And while the batting changed to accommodate the need for large scores, the bowling changed too. One-day cricket created the necessity for the bowling side to concentrate on keeping the scoring in check instead of trying to get batsmen out. The intention in test matches was to bowl out an entire side twice in a match, but in one-day cricket, it was to restrict the other side's score and to keep them from scoring runs.

This meant that bowlers were no longer bowling imaginatively in an attempt to get wickets, but rather on maintaining a particular line and length in order to restrict the scoring. The alternative was to bowl bouncers and rely on blinding pace. This pace and bouncers approach may have worked in the initial years of the WSC and one-day cricket, but as the game evolved, and a limit to the number of bouncers bowled was imposed, the most effective one-day bowlers emerged as those who could maintain a rigorous discipline in their bowling with respect to line and length.[18] Memon argues that because of this need to restrict batsmen, bowlers in one-day cricket 'have taken a backseat to batsmen'. Several commentators believed that this new format of the game rang the death knell for practitioners of the art of spin bowling. In fact, in the years directly after the WSC and the first few World Cups, there was a sharp decline in the 'quality and quantity' of spin bowlers. Memon quotes Bishen Singh Bedi, the grandmaster of spin bowling, as having said, 'It is this wretched one-day game which has ruined our spinners' during India's tour of England in 1990. The fear that an over of spin bowling can prove to be expensive in a one-day game restricted spinners from deviating too much from the line and length routine.

Memon quotes from Mike Brearley's book, *Art of Captaincy*, to conjecture that the reason spin bowlers had all but vanished from the scene in the two decades following the introduction of one-day cricket is because of the way the pitches and fields were made. The use of fertilizers, the watering of the outfield, and even changes in the method of manufacture of the cricket balls, in Bearley's opinion, were all of the assistance to seamers. Ravi Shastri, who rose to fame as a batsman and all-rounder, began his career as a spin bowler. He acknowledged in an interview with Ayaz Memon that the one-day game was responsible for the disappearance of the spinners. Shastri said that this is because the one-day game was essentially a batsman's game. He also said that bowlers did not concentrate on taking wickets, because the primary purpose of the bowler was containment and the fielding restrictions make it very difficult anyway. The art and the guile of the spinner became a luxury that a team could ill afford in an innings of 50-overs, since the implications of letting a batsman score runs while gunning for his wicket are far too risky in this format of the game.

Another aspect of change in the game was the quality of fielding and running between the wickets. As the need for scoring quick runs became important, so did the need to run ever more effectively between the wickets. In exactly the same manner, the importance of containment was making fielding a more dangerous job than ever before. Sliding, diving, chasing, tumbling after the ball became ever more important, because sometimes a run saved, in the words of Memon, 'became twice as priceless as a run scored'. This sort of action on the field also added to the entertainment factor of this new fast format of instant cricket. Commenting on how this new enthusiasm for fielding finds the players' whites no longer spotless at the end of the day, Memon observes that 'financial rewards which follow take adequate care of increased laundry bills'.

All this, coupled with the fact that the primary purpose of Packer's series was to *entertain* audiences, both in stadia and through the television, led to enormous changes in standard game-play. It was for this reason that what began as a series of 'super tests' ultimately found its niche in the faster-paced one-day game. Reflecting on this aspect of WSC, Martin Williamson writes, 'It was all about big hitting and fast bowlers. Spinners or grafters hardly got a look in. It was brutal ...' Bouncers became a norm and the traditional ban on bowling short to tail-enders was no longer a rule. In one especially horrific incident, David Hookes suffered a broken jaw at the hands of an Andy Roberts delivery. Williamson conjectures that this incident might have speeded up the arrival of helmets (an interesting piece of technology) on the cricket pitch.[19] *Wisden* magazine quotes Tony Greig from an article in the *Sun Herald* on the issue:

> The competition in WSC is so intense; teams can no longer afford to allow the opposition tail-enders to hang around. Consequently the pace bowlers are dishing out an unprecedented amount of bouncers to the 'rabbits'. So it is pleasing to see that cricketers like Dennis Lillee and Garth le Roux have got the message, swallowed their pride, and are wearing helmets.[20]

The advent of the helmet too was a cause for much debate. Traditionalists believed that heavy weather was being made of the increased pace in the bowling attack, and that several great batsmen had played pace before without the need for helmets. Trevor Bailey, the English all-rounder, writing in *Wisden*, remembers with nostalgia the times when a batsman at the crease could be identified from the stands because of his stance, build, headgear or hair, and laments the changing times. He writes:

> Who could have failed to pick out Cyril Washbrook with his cap at a jaunty angle, or Jack Robertson, who wore his with the precision of a guardsman? Then again, there was the hairstyles of Herbert Sutcliffe, black patent-leather glinting in the sun, complete with the straightest of partings, the blonde waves of Joe Hardstaff, Reg Simpson's dark curls, and Denis Compton's, so unlike those Brylcreem advertisements, forever unruly. Today, as often as not, it is impossible to tell

who is batting without first consulting a scorecard, so many players being encrusted in helmets and camouflaged by visors. This gives them a space-age image, devoid of individuality and as dull as dirty denims.[21]

Bailey goes on to express surprise at the fact that ever since players have been wearing helmets, the incidence of them being hit has increased. He dismisses the theory that this is because of the increase in fast and medium-paced bowling. According to him, because of the extra protection that players now had, they were less worried, and were attempting to hook or play deliveries that they otherwise would not have attempted such shots at. And in doing so, they were not moving as quickly as they otherwise should have and were consequently getting hit. But the helmet, like much else from the WSC 'circus', was here to stay. While pads for batsmen had existed before, several other kinds of safety equipment like helmets and elbow guards increasingly began to be seen on the cricket field; and have now become conventional for any cricketer.

A Shifting Centre

What was once derided as 'pyjama cricket' soon became the standard order of play. With the commercial success of the World Cups—arguably cricket's first (but not last) import from the world of football—the format of the one-day game was given the legitimacy it lacked hitherto. The next steps for cricket—more innovations in the game itself and a deeper relationship with technology—seem almost predictable in hindsight. From playing equipment to umpiring, from diet plans for players to appointing full-time psychotherapists for teams, and from innovative advertising hoardings in stadia to the kind of television and other coverage that cricket received, technological knowhow and innovations crept into practically every aspect of the game, sponsored by the revenue generated by using cricket as an advertising platform.

While technology has swept through most sports, the game of cricket has perhaps been most emphatically and profoundly re-shaped and re-structured. From being a game that was played over the better part of a week, it has now become like almost every other sport in terms of time taken to wrap up a match. In this, the change in cricket has been most significant. Writing of the newest form of cricket—Twenty20—in a 2008 article in *The Telegraph*, historian Ramachandra Guha writes, 'The pleasures of the shortest game are intense but also wholly ephemeral'.[22] He likens test cricket to 'the finest scotch', one-day games to Indian Made Foreign liquor (IMFL) and the Twenty20 game to 'local hooch', and expresses his disdain at the new format by writing, 'The addict who cannot have the first or the second will make do with the last'. Expanding the metaphor, he goes on to say:

> As compared to Twenty20, 50-50 allows a greater exposure to the varieties and subtleties of the game. After spending a whole day at the cricket ground, one can, as it were, remember individual sips of the drink that one has consumed. On the other hand, after a Twenty20 game, all one remembers is that one got drunk, and one's side won, or lost.

Test cricket was peculiar in all these respects, primarily because of the slowness of the game itself. Liberally peppered with drinks breaks, lunch, tea, and the gaps between overs, the principal intention of playing test cricket did not always appear to be to solely win or lose. The game itself was, in effect, structured in a manner that allowed for slowness to characterize play. Elaborate strategizing, the practice of 'placing the field' in a specific way for specific batsmen off the bowling of specific bowlers on specific days, required considerable time and thought on the field, while the match was on. This sort of detailed involvement in every ball bowled appears to have been one of the reasons C.L.R. James compared cricket to theatre and ballet more than to other sports.[23]

The changes in the game that have been spurred by technology—be it the television and related inventions, sports medicine, training equipment, or even software for analysis and broadcast innovations such as the internet and social networking—have taken cricket from being a game to becoming a platform for several new constituencies. After Kerry Packer brought television into mainstream cricket, the influx of technology has shaped the way cricket has been engaged with. The latest innovation in cricket has been the emergence of Twenty20 cricket. Providing an alternative for television viewers from prime-time

TV, and presented as a reality show packaged with celebrities from the worlds of business, cinema, and cricket; the new format of the game is a further injection of speed into the game, once again through the syringe of technology.

Cricket, thus, has been transformed into an industry, on which ride several other interests and stakeholders. Software engineers who can design better analytical software, film stars who seek publicity, players looking for quick money, businesses looking for a better advertising platform, and television channels trying to improve their ratings—are all stakeholders in the game of cricket today. The game itself is no longer the centre of the event of the match. With all the diverse interests riding on the match, cricket as a sport seems to have developed several foci around which it is played. In this de-centred universe, the game is just one of many centres that are important. The direction in which cricket moves is determined by the strength of these several, unaligned, diverse focal points and the mutual push and pull that they can exert on the game of cricket. In comparison to being the sport that Ashis Nandy described as a 'ritualised garden party',[24] cricket is today, first and foremost, a platform. Mediated as it is by technology, cricket has proved to be an excellent vessel for the promotion, development, and sustenance of several other industries.

2

Cricket at the Altar of Technology

On 15 May 1999, as India and South Africa began their respective World
Cup campaigns in England at the County Ground in Hove, Sussex; television viewers had a ring-side view of an interesting technology-related
controversy. After getting away unnoticed in some benefit matches earlier
in the year and in a warm-up match before the World Cup, South Africa's
captain Hansie Cronje and fast bowler Alan Donald were wearing small
earpieces on the field to allow them to hear instructions from the coach,
Bob Woolmer, in the dressing room.[1] It was the television commentators
who first noticed the earpieces. And then Indian opener Sourav Ganguly
spotted them and brought them to the attention of the on-field umpires
just before the first drinks break.

Bob Woolmer, before coming up with the plan to wear earpieces,
had ensured that they were not in direct contravention of any of the
rules of the ICC. When the on-field umpires—Steve Bucknor and
David Shepherd—spoke to a candid Cronje about the earpiece,
they could not decide whether it was legal or not, and called in the
Match Referee Talat Ali to adjudicate. When he could not decide either, the matter went further up the ladder to the ICC. After much
deliberation, the apex cricket body decided that while the earpieces
were not flouting any of the written rules, they were unfair. Ali conveyed the message to the South Africans during the drinks break, and
Cronje and Donald were made to get rid of their earpieces. While this
entire episode was relayed in detail to the audiences watching the match
on TV, spectators in the stadium were left—as Martin Williamson calls
it—'bemused' because the earpieces were too small to be noticed by anyone in the stands.

Speeding up Sport. Vidya Subramanian, Oxford University Press. © Oxford University Press 2022.
DOI: 10.1093/oso/9780192865120.003.0003

Opening the Floodgates

The upshot of the event, of course, was that the ICC banned the use of such devices. But Bob Woolmer remained optimistic about the chances of using such technology in the future. Even rival captain—India's Mohammad Azharuddin—was of the opinion that this was bound to happen. He is quoted to have said, 'It's going to happen ... It does in other sports'. The incident also marks the increasing dependence of cricket players on the team's coach. Traditionally, a coach was merely the person who took care of the team equipment and managed net practice sessions. Cricket historian and writer Gideon Haigh comments[2] on this marked difference between conventional cricket and other sports when he says,

> Every other sport knelt at the altar of the coach, manager or guru; in cricket, despite a technical rigour and complexity that begat so many instructional books, the captain remained all-powerful. The game, as it were, was learned without formally being taught.

Haigh goes on to write about the television being an important impetus in the development of the coach as one of the central members of a team. With the advent of videography, replays and the ability to repeatedly (and in slow motion) watch individual actions of every player, the job of the coach came to include studying every player and advising each one accordingly. The smallest details of the stance of a batsman, the arm action of a bowler, or the dive of a fielder became more open to scrutiny, and consequently more malleable to training. Bob Woolmer's work with South Africa, John Wright's and Gary Kirsten's with India, and Duncan Fletcher's with England are some of several examples in international cricket of the importance of the coach.

Haigh's insight into the link between the increase in television coverage and its direct impact in increasing the influence of the coach in an extended cricket team provides a great starting point for the analysis of the changing role of the coach in cricket. Cricket analyst Peter English seems to agree with this notion as he points out the expansion of the role of the coach to official ranks towards the end of the twentieth century.[3] From being the person who doubled up as a manager, the coach today commands the services of a large team that supervises the training of the team. But the importance of this role as a coach is not something that has met with universal approval. Former players such as Ian Chappell and Shane Warne have decried the importance of intensive coaching, having been vocal about their opinion that the best players do not need constant nurturing and an 'occasional re-pointing in the right direction' should suffice. But as English rightly points out, they are in the minority. John Buchanan—a teacher by trade and a one-time university lecturer[4]—as Australia's coach has been widely credited with the success of the world-beating outfit that Australia is. It was under his coaching that Australia won the 2007 World Cup. Others, including Warne and Chappell, have described Buchanan as 'someone with the most fortunate timing in the game', crediting his success to a team of great players who would have dominated world cricket anyway. In 1998, when he was coaching the Middlesex county team, they ranked 17th—their lowest ever—in the County Championship. He was then accused of 'over-complicating a simple game'.

In an interview, Gideon Haigh[5] wondered if, perhaps, the increasing role of the coach had not actually made players 'less independent'. 'There's a kind of learned helplessness about them. If the coach doesn't tell them what to do, then they don't really know. They don't respond ... they don't withstand pressure in the way that previous generations of players have withstood it', he said. He wondered if the T20 mode of play had made players more reliant on coaches, more aggressive (as the format demanded) but also perhaps more brittle.

Shaping the Game

Even as the naysayers argued against the merits of a full-time coach, the fact of every national team having not just a coach but an entire coaching squad is proof of the victors in this debate. Zach Hitchcock, a software engineer by profession and a successful video analyst for the New Zealand cricket team, created for the team a system called Feedback Cricket in 1999 to log data that could be used later for analysis. Initially met with resistance from the New Zealand players, the technology gradually gained acceptance. Batsmen used the software to analyse their dismissals and review the need to make changes and work on nuances in their game at the nets, in consultation with the batting coach and the physiotherapist. Bowlers used it to analyse their actions in frame-by-frame detail, and look at individual deliveries so they could build on what they are doing right and what kinks need to be ironed out.[6]

In an interview with S. Ramakrishnan,[7] Director of the Chennai-based sports analytics firm Sports Mechanics,[8] (conducted in 2010–11, while I was working on my MPhil) he stressed the contribution of technology in sports training. He believes that technology in coaching and training is here to stay, and by the use of technology from the start of a player's career, it is possible to produce players of a far superior quality. At the time that I was writing my doctoral thesis in 2015, Sports Mechanics provided players who signed up with them the option of videographing their gameplay and technique to provide online consulting and coaching to improve performance. The company also provided existing teams 'actionable intelligence' through analysis of 'data and video based information'. The website promised to[9]

> ensure (that) our state-of-the-art analysis systems, dedicated back end analytics and fan engagement systems, IT and technical development teams work together to deliver a faster, better platform which yields stronger results and actionable insights for your team. In some cases we also send front end analysts from our pool of experience professionals to assist your team physically and deliver our services in a more personalized way.

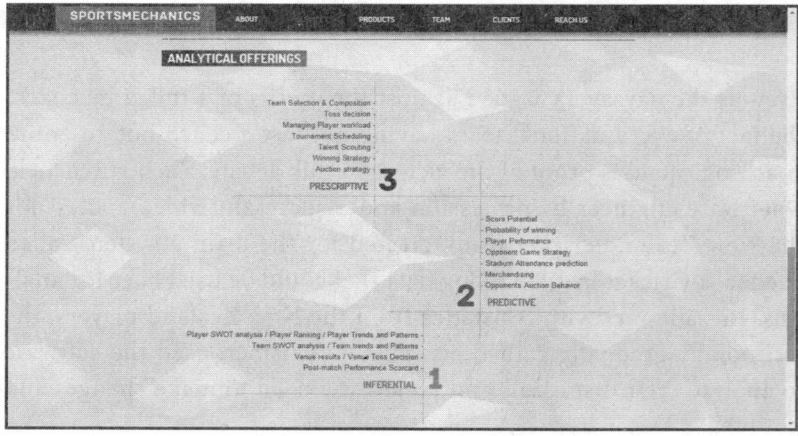

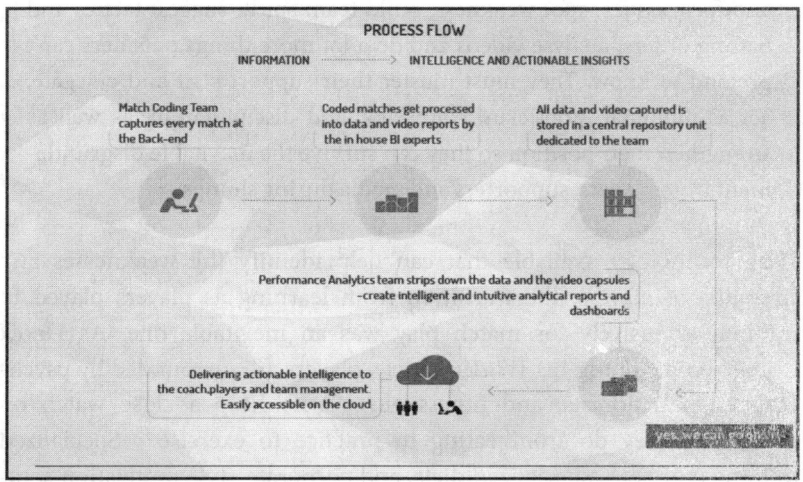

The company aims to bring together a team of coaches, physiotherapists, and 'industry-envied cricketing domain experts coupled with a right blend of technical professionals providing the best of the solutions—a video based online mentoring platform' and 'focuses on bringing in accelerated learning technologies to acquire skill sets and performance enhancements by offering e-learning capabilities to athletes, coaches and institutions to effectively govern, manage, (and) analyze'.[10]

The 'Clientele' page of the website gave an indication of the reach that this technological tool had in the world of cricket, even in 2015. From administrative bodies of international cricket teams such as India and Sri Lanka and state cricket associations of Tamil Nadu and Rajasthan to bodies such as the ICC High Performance Programme and several Indian Premier League (IPL) teams, the company lists a large number of state level, national, and international sporting bodies as clients who have used these technological services in the areas of coaching and training.[11] This indicates a marked shift in the way new players are learning the sport too. And incorporating these technologies within the ambit of coaching makes the coach's role into what Peter English calls 'the most convoluted in the game'. English describes the role of a coach in the modern cricket team as:

They are expected to run complex training sessions tailored to each discipline, advise the decision-makers on their charges' mental, physical and form issues, spot weakness, build team spirit, suggest tactics and batting orders, analyse videos and do a lot more things outsiders can't pretend to know. They must muster their support staff and delegate, act as diplomat, politician, counsellor and disciplinarian, as well as strengthen their position so they can survive the inevitable disgruntlement from players, supporters and media during slumps.[12]

With technology available that can help identify the weaknesses and strengths of players, the transition from learning as players played to training extensively for match play was an inevitable one. As Derek Pringle points out in his *Wisden* article, players are surrounded by psychologists, nutritionists, and fitness gurus who keep a close watch on everything they do from eating to practice to exercise.[13] Specialized training regimens, specialized diets, and corporate-style motivation seminars are crafted for individual players as they focus on honing necessary skills. The cricket industry has thus made room for software engineers, former players, and a host of other professionals to become a part of it. All this has spawned several entirely new industries that piggyback on popular sports. Sports analytics is one of them. Combining video recordings, software skills, medicine, nutrition, and optionally a prior interest in the game, the analytics industry is just one of the many things that ride on cricket.

In an interview with former India spin bowler and current television commentator Murali Kartik, he exclaimed on the advances that technology had made even in the areas of nutrition. In the 1990s, he told me, when India was touring Pakistan, he had a terrible time with available food and ended up losing a lot of weight on that single tour. The reason was that he is a strict vegetarian and vegetarian food was not easy to come by in Pakistan. 'Even the *dal* (lentils) had meat in it', he said.[14] This is no longer a problem that any international cricketer would face. The team of nutritionists, physiotherapists, etc. that accompanies a team would ensure that the diet and nutritional needs of each player—calculated and measured—were available to every member of the team at all times.

Kartik's enthusiastic endorsement of technological advancements is at odds with some other commentators of the game. Derek Pringle fears that the growing influence of science in cricket may be a response to its guilty conscience. He says, 'It will not guarantee better results, but at least it shows that the game is willing to respond to external pressures'. He goes on to question the legitimacy of 'this no-stone-unturned pact with science' and reflects, almost melancholically that 'science can only try to create ever-efficient machines out of players. This is a game whose appeal relies on its unpredictability. They may be able to clone sheep. Eleven Ian Bothams would keep the bar well and truly propped up after play, but they would not make the game any more intoxicating'.[15]

The Omniscient Camera

The changes that took place in the realm of coaching happened away from the limelight and television screens. But one of the more glaring impacts of technology in cricket can be seen in the more prominent aspect of umpiring, placing the hitherto sacrosanct place of the umpire under the microscope and opening up on-field umpiring decisions to scrutiny and evaluation, making umpiring one of the most technologically enhanced aspects of the game. As a direct result of slow-motion television replays that everyone—from television commentators to viewers at home and players in dressing rooms—had access to, the bad decisions (and some close ones that the on-field umpires missed) were noticed far more than before and commented on widely. Writes Mukul Kesavan, albeit in a different context, on the increasing use of technology in umpiring:

> Cricket ... has moved from a system of supervision based on an acceptance of human (read umpiring) error and the alleged honour of the gentleman cricketer, to an umpiring regime dependent on (and second-guessed by) the omniscient camera.[16]

In place of expecting the 'gentleman cricketer' to take in his stride any perceived umpiring errors or expecting him to 'walk' when out, cricket and cricketers began to demand (and receive) proof of the fallibility of the on-field umpire. As far back as in 1983, an editorial in *Wisden* spoke of how much more exacting the job of the umpire had become. 'Partly because of all the money that is at stake ... and by no means least because of television, the man in the white coat is now under constant pressure', reads the Editorial.[17] As a result of this pressure, both on the umpires and the administrators of the game to *improve* the *quality* of umpiring, in 1992, the television was integrated into the official umpiring framework. The 'Third Umpire' was a revolutionary change in the way umpiring decisions were made.

Compare this to a problem that made many headlines during the English tour of India in 1972–73, when the touring English side still played as the Marylebone Cricket Club or the MCC. After four tests in Delhi, Calcutta, Madras, and Kanpur, the fifth test was to be played in Bombay in February 1973, and a particular attitude of the players of both sides was making news. Purists and pundits frowned upon it, young players were increasingly making it a norm, and as it is with every new generation, the older generation was making its displeasure known.

The problem, as it were, was what one journalist called 'undermining the umpire's authority'.[18] 'Tendentious appealing' and 'umpire baiting' became important sidelights of a series in which India's fielding and spin bowling prowess were the centre of a lot of positive attention. The English, having been at the receiving end of what they felt were two bad umpiring decisions in the Delhi test, resorted to loud and as some commentators saw it, intimidating appealing. The Indian side saw it as trying to bully the umpire into deciding in their favour. They, in turn, with the support of the sizeable crowds behind them, reciprocated in kind. Commentators were quick to express their displeasure at this retaliatory appealing that the Indians resorted to, and the resultant unpleasantness that marred the series.

In the third test at Madras, when Ajit Wadekar was caught by Tony Greig in the slips off Chris Old, the umpire did not immediately give the batsman out, apparently unsighted by Old cutting across in his follow-through. After some demonstration by the fielding side and a word with the other umpire, the appeal was upheld. Raju Bharatan in *The Illustrated Weekly of India* described the situation as 'ugly' and commented on how the entire situation could have been averted had Wadekar simply, to use a cricketing term, 'walked'. Wadekar, for his part, explained later that he was not sure that Greig's appeal held water, even though the catch had been caught at a knee-high level. Bharatan expresses surprise that the two teams had not already got together to discuss the situation and sorted out this 'human problem' by agreeing to a code of conduct to avoid such unseemly behaviour. This was simply not cricket.

Unaided by the technology of a television umpire, and in the absence of the possibility of viewing the contentious moment in a frame-by-frame visual from every imaginable angle, the onus of the decision rested entirely with the on-field umpire. And his decision—even in those heady, modern days where critics shook their heads at the irreverence of the new breed of cricketers—depended on the conduct of the players. Cricket was played in a deeply moral universe; one in which if a player thought he was out, he was expected to 'walk' whether or not the umpire ruled so, and if a catch was contentious, the catcher's word was the last word on the issue. There were rules, and then there were rules. The written rules of the game were, of course, adhered to. But there was this other set of unwritten rules, which was also important. Ashis Nandy, in *The Tao of Cricket*, speaks of how the first ring of spectators for a cricketer was the players on the field.[19] To be caught cheating or hustling by them was a matter of great embarrassment. A batting landmark such as a fifty or a century was applauded by members of the fielding side as the accepted thing to do. 'You play with the opposition as well as against them', says Scyld Berry in *Wisden* 2008.[20] The crowd at the stadium was only the second ring of viewers—a representative cross section of the society that counted. This view, says Nandy, 'kept up the pressure on a player to conform' to the moral guidelines of cricket—what Nandy terms 'inner norms' of the game.

Traditionally, cricket as embodied by the Victorian era was, as Nandy describes it, 'on one plane a violent battle which by common consent had to be played like a genteel, ritualised garden party, at another a profession which had to be practised as a pastime'.[21] And when the 'violent battle' aspect came to the surface, the purists always frowned upon it. Although the kind of disregard for the unwritten traditions of the game seen in the appealing row—even in the seventies—was certainly not a new phenomenon, it was serious enough to invite comment. The contrast to behaviour in other sports such as baseball (a close relative of cricket) is brought out by C.L.R. James in his eminently readable book *Beyond a Boundary*. He describes an encounter he had with baseball in the United States. As he watched a baseball match with some friends, he expresses outrage at the 'howls of anger and rage and denunciation which they hurled at the players as a matter of course'. He goes on to express deep distress and shock at the fact that managers and players 'protested against adverse decisions' as though it were routine, 'and sometimes, after bitter quarrels, were ordered off the field, fined, and punished in other ways'.[22]

He goes on to describe how he once played a game of cricket with these friends after explaining the rules to them. He writes of the game,

> As soon as the fielders took position, they burst out with hue and cry, and when a ball was hit towards a fieldsman his own side seemed to pursue him like the hounds of heaven until he had gathered the ball and thrown it in. All this seemed natural to them. It was very strange to me.

Elsewhere in the book, James, talking of the brilliance of the West Indian player Wilton St. Hill's ability to play the leg-glance, describes a match at the Queen's Park Oval in Trinidad in 1926. It provides an interesting contrast to the baseball story above. As St. Hill batted in sublime form, Yorkshireman Percy Holmes was fielding at deep third-man and on the boundary behind the bowler. James writes,

> St. Hill had him running now thirty yards for the on-drive and then the other way for the off-drive ... The Yorkshireman never relaxed for an instant and chased each ball like a hare, but he had the time and strength to talk to us and admire this superlative batting. Each time St. Hill made a stroke, we could see Holmes smile as he ducked his head to chase the ball.

Trial by TV

Cricket, in that era, seems to have been located in a moral universe, where the word of a fielder decided a boundary, and batsmen who did not 'walk' when they knew they were out were frowned upon and cited as bad examples. And since the decisions of the field could not be referred to the all-seeing eye of the television camera, the umpire's word was law and was treated with a respect that a scheme such as the 'Umpire Decision Review System' seems to belie. In the technologically unmediated game of this time, contraptions such as the stump vision camera, the Snickometer, Hawk-Eye, and the third television umpire* were not only unheard of, but also seemed unnecessary to the game.

In this displacement of the moral centre from the player to the camera, technology has become the backdrop of the game. And the invisible rules of cricket appear to have been replaced with the diktat of the all-seeing eye of the television camera and slow-motion replays. Technologically mediated cricket does not need a fielder to vouch for a boundary or to claim a clean catch; the all-seeing eye provides the necessary proof, removing the

---

* The television umpire or third umpire is the off-field umpire to whom decisions are referred when the on-field umpires are not sure of the decision. He has the benefit of television replays and several camera angles to take the decision of whether a batsman is out or not. His decision is conveyed to the field through the stadium scorecard or through red and green lights (red for 'out', green for 'not out').

onus of fair play from the player and shifting it in its entirety to techno-logically mediated umpiring.

The third off-field umpire, who has the benefit of television replays to help him make decisions that on-field umpires are not sure of and have the option of referring to the 'television umpire', was inducted into cricket on the recommendation of the Sri Lankan journalist Mahinda Wijesinghe and has been an integral part of cricket matches since 1992.[23] Ranjit Fernando, a former Sri Lankan cricketer, defends the need for the third umpire. Reflecting the opinion of John Woodcock, Editor of *Wisden* in 1983, Fernando refers to how much—pride and money—is at stake in every match, and calls it 'natural' for players to want to win 'by hook or by crook'. In such a situation, he writes, 'the think-tank at the helm had to devise a method to eradicate mistakes, or, at least, minimise them'. He attributes this need as the cause of the introduction of the television um-pire. Since then, the third umpire has been a permanent addition to inter-national cricket matches.

The tools that a television umpire has to work with are, interestingly, those that were first introduced to cricket as part of the entertainment value additions for television viewers—the 'slow-motion replay', Hawk-Eye, the snickometer, and HotSpot. In an experiment in 2004, stump microphones were linked to earpieces that were given to umpires to ensure better deci-sions aided by technology.[24] The snickometer, Hawk-Eye and about 30 on-field cameras have changed the way umpires interact with the game.

The snickometer, popularly called 'Snicko', was invented by Allan Plaskett, an English scientist. This technology was first used in 1999 by Channel 4 in England to aid commentators.[25] The snickometer is a com-bination of a very sensitive microphone placed in one of the stumps and an oscilloscope that measures sound waves which is connected to the mi-crophone. When the ball nicks the bat, the oscilloscope picks up the sound waves. Simultaneously, a high-speed camera records the passing of the ball. The recorded waves from the oscilloscope are then shown side by side with the slow-motion video of the ball's path. The shape of the sound wave and the position of the bat and ball at that instant help determine whether the sound seems to come from the bat hitting the ball or some other object.[26]

HotSpot too is an innovation that made its way into gameplay via com-mentators on television. It made its debut during the first match of the Ashes in 2006–07 at the Gabba in Brisbane, Australia. This technology uses infrared camera technology to determine which part of the batsman's body or bat made contact with the ball. Two powerful thermal-imaging cameras are placed around the field—behind the bowler's arm at each end. These cameras identify and calculate the amount of heat generated by the impact of the ball against another object. According to *ESPNCricinfo*, 'computer technology then generates a negative image on which the point of contact is highlighted as a red friction "hot spot"'. The technology used in HotSpot was originally developed for tracking tanks and fighter jet aircraft in the military.[27]

Hawk-Eye, the system that—by recreating a bowled ball's possible trajectory—aids in making leg before wicket (lbw) decisions more accurate, uses technology from missile guidance systems. Upto six cameras positioned around the stadium capture the trajectory, flight, speed, and movement of the ball from the bowler's hand to the point it bounces on the pitch, and then from the instant it bounces off the pitch to the moment it makes contact with the batsman's pad or his bat.[28] It then predicts what would have happened if the ball had not been stopped; and charts the remaining path towards and beyond the stumps. This is not technology replaying what has already transpired for a better view. This is technology indulging in conjecture by predicting possibilities.

While the use of such technology has largely been applauded by experts and laymen alike, several questions about its accuracy too have been raised, not just in cricket but in sports such as tennis as well, where Hawk-Eye is now par for the course. Roger Federer, the champion tennis player from Switzerland, has been an outspoken opponent of the system, having been at the wrong end of an obvious error by the machine during the Wimbledon finals of 2007.[29]

Human Error and Technological Infallibility

Harry Collins and Robert Evans have discussed the advertised margins of error by the company that provides Hawk-Eye technology, and conclude that since the advertised margin is an 'average' of 3.6 millimetres, it stands to reason that there are occasions when the margin of error can be much greater.

The paper notes that for lbw decisions, for several years after the introduction of Hawk-Eye into television broadcasts of cricket, 'cricket commentators would simply remark on what Hawk-Eye showed on the screen, giving the impression, perhaps inadvertently, that the virtual reality represented exactly what would actually have happened had the pad not been struck'. The authors focus on the public understanding of the technology and provide insight into the eventual acceptance of the technology as an improvement over the on-field umpire due to a lack of deeper understanding of the nuances of the technology. The authors even go so far as to suggest that it would be more responsible of commentators to remark that, ' "Hawk-Eye was 99.9% sure the ball was going to hit the wicket so the umpire was right," or "Hawk-Eye was only 90% sure the ball was going to hit the wicket—the umpire should not have given it out" '.

Umpire Dickie Bird too agreed that the new technology is not as infallible as many seem to think. He is quoted to have said that 'Hawk-Eye cannot tell the state of the pitch, the bounce of the ball and how much it has swung or seamed. I reckon balls that are shown to be clipping leg stump would in fact miss it by 18 inches'.[30]

An example of the fallibility of this technologically mediated umpiring was seen in the 2014 edition of the IPL. In this edition of the IPL, the first part of the season was played in the UAE due to elections in India and the reluctance of the Indian government to divert security forces to the IPL during the polls.[31]

It was during the 14th match of the season held in Abu Dhabi. In what is a very rare occurrence for an IPL match, the Rajasthan Royals rounded up the much vaunted batting line-up of (what was then) Vijay Mallya's Royal Challengers Bangalore (RCB) for all of 70 runs in the first innings. As the Rajasthan Royals worked slowly and unhurriedly towards the lowest total in that edition of the IPL, they were at 60-3 in the 12th over. In the fourth ball of the over, Abhishek Nayar was making heavy weather of what should have been an easy three runs off Ashok Dinda. As he got back to the batsman's crease at full stretch, diving to make it, Parthiv Patel, RCB's wicketkeeper, took off the bails, leading to loud appeals for a runout.

It looked possible, but it was too close for the on-field umpire to call. The 'third umpire' brought up the relevant camera angles, but it still was not clear if Nayar had made it past the crease before Patel took off the bails. Harsha Bhogle and Rameez Raja, the commentators, could not agree whether it was out or not. But they agreed that the longer the third umpire took, the better were chances of a 'not-out' call. The first frame had Nayar's bat slightly short of the crease and the bails firmly in place, and the next frame showed Nayar's bat well (enough) inside the crease and the bails off.[32] Had there been a frame between these two, it may have been easier to make the call. 'He has been saved by a frame', read the ball-by-ball commentary on the *ESPNCricinfo* webpage.

With all the technology available in the match and all the possible camera angles, it was one of those moments that brought to the fore the inadequacy and fallibility of the technologies that are always discussed—at least in the commentary box—as almost superhuman or infallible.

Ivo Tennant believes that all these technologies go a long way in undermining the authority of the umpires.[33] He seems to suggest that with all the available technologies to *aid* umpiring, the umpire himself may become obsolete. And that is a debate that is far from being laid to rest in the present day.

It is important to note that all these technologies that are now available to the 'television umpire', should a decision be referred to them, came into the game via television programming for the sport—technologies that were sometimes borrowed from the military, and costing millions in research and development. In an attempt to make the sport on television purportedly 'more interesting', several innovations are added. Ivo Tennant expresses a conviction that all this 'techno wizardry' enhances the 'enjoyment and appreciation of television viewers' and quotes Paul King, executive producer of Sky Sports, as saying that these technologies 'provide genuine benefit for viewers and our commentators rather than just being there for the sake of it'.

Testing Technology

Although Tennant concedes that the Sky Network does not obtain feedback about whether or not such technology and the resulting pleasure and knowledge obtained through them was significant in the viewers' decisions to renew their subscriptions, he points out that there do not appear to have been any outrage or complaints about them either. But the mass media world being driven by numbers and statistics as it is, it is the number of people that have seen a specific bit of programming that is more important than the depth of their pleasure or understanding. Other writing on the subject has spoken of how the television has bettered the game by making it easier to see the game more clearly than one might in a stadium, and how the television experience creates a sense of greater identification with the game by means of contests[34] and other peripheral activities (such as live tweeting, etc.) that make viewing more participatory.

Tennant also talks of the amount of investment and the range of technology that goes into the coverage of a single cricket match. In reference to Sky Sports, which has been providing cricket coverage in high definition (HD) since 2006, he describes the use of more than 30 cameras, including one in the commentary box, stump cameras, and extra ones for special 3D coverage, more than 40 microphones, 15 miles of cabling, an on-site production crew of 80 people, and an average of 15 trucks, which arrive at the cricket ground two entire days before the start of play. In addition, there is the director's truck, which he says is 'the largest vehicle permitted on roads in Britain'. This vehicle includes 78 screens and takes around four hours to 'de-rig'.[35]

Cricket is one of the few sports that have embraced the advance of technology into the game quite readily as compared to others such as football or tennis. While some may argue that readiness to embrace change and accept new technology is a good thing and the game has evolved to greater heights because of it, there have been doubts that perhaps cricket may have adopted certain technologies a bit too quickly. Paul Hawkins, the founder of Hawk-Eye, has suggested that perhaps cricket administrators had been too hasty in incorporating Hawk-Eye into cricket decision making, and perhaps adopted the technology without having conducted sufficient trials.[36]

Speaking during the 2013 Ashes series in which technology related controversies created headlines alongside England's victories, Hawkins said, 'What cricket hasn't done as much as other sports is test anything'. He was speaking at the launch of football's first step into technologically assisted officiating at the Emirates Stadium in London. He went on to say, 'This (football's Goal Decision System) has been very, very heavily tested whereas cricket's hasn't really undergone any testing. It's almost like it has tested it in live conditions so they are inheriting broadcast technology rather than developing officiating technology'. This is an important critique of the manner in which technology has been adopted into cricket. Since the needs and aspirations of broadcast are not (and some might say, should not) always be the same as that of on-field decision making and officiating; it stands to reason that the technologies developed for the two must be independently researched and extensively tested, especially in the case of on-field officiating.

The 2013 Ashes series was also marred by controversy regarding the Decision Review System and disputed allegations that players may have been adding extra layers of silicone tape to their bats to escape detection by the HotSpot system.[37] Players in cricket are allowed to use tape on their bats to protect and repair them, and fibreglass tape has been used for this purpose. The allegation was that since silicone has low thermal conductivity, silicone tape could reduce the heat transfer and friction produced when the bat hits the ball, thus rendering HotSpot unable to see a thermal 'hot spot' at the point of impact of slight nicks. However, no evidence was produced to confirm that this had indeed occurred. The system, though, came in for much criticism from experts and media alike,[38] once again highlighting the need for more and better testing within the sport.

Broadcast technology itself has undergone a sea change in recent years. Apart from adding what can be called umpiring aids, the technology for broadcast itself has changed, catering as it does to several different modes of viewing. From simply broadcasting for television, second screen (laptops and computers) and third screen (mobile phones) experiences have become extremely important for sports. The increasing number of people watching or following sport not just on computer screens, but on mobile phones has increased dramatically in recent years. The number of internet users worldwide has increased from 360 million in 2000 to almost 5 billion in 2020[39] (an almost 14-fold increase). Almost 52% of these users live in Asia, but the internet penetration rate* in Asia is less

---

* According to *Internet World Stats*, 'The Internet Penetration Rate corresponds to the percentage of the total population of a given country or region that uses the Internet'. The definition of 'Internet Users' is given as: 'Anyone currently in capacity to use the Internet. There are two requirements for a person to be considered an Internet User: (1) The person must have available access to an Internet connection point, and (2) The person must have the basic knowledge required to use web technology.

than 60%. According to the Internet and Mobile Association of India (IAMAI),[40] there are 504 million internet users in India, with an internet penetration of only 36%, but the number is significant because programming such as that of the IPL is targeted specifically to appeal to this demographic. As a comparison, in the United States alone—which has an internet penetration rate of almost 90%—there are a total of only 297 million users (as reported in October 2020).

Sport is an important and growing cluster online, particularly with the increasing popularity of video streaming services and the increase in internet speeds to enable uninterrupted live streaming of important events. With new additions such as viewers being able to switch camera angles while watching online (slip-view, for example), the technologies involved in the production and distribution of sport content have completely changed the way the sport is viewed and engaged with.

Instant Cricket

The story of the evolution of cricket is one that is punctuated by several ruptures in the flow of the narrative. From Kerry Packer's World Series Cricket (more on that in Chapter 3) to the birth of the IPL, every radical transformation in the game seems to have come from forces outside the game seeking a foothold within it, usually attempting to induct novelties into the game, whether or not enriching the sport itself. The presence of numerous 24-hour sports channels has been linked to an increasing viewership that has, in turn, been linked to providing a greater involvement for viewers with the game, and consequently 'enriching' the experience of cricket. Television using sports programming to increase profit margins is a well-known fact and it would not be incorrect to conjecture that it may well be called an impetus to National Boards to increase the amount of cricket (or in fact, any sport) played for television.

Boria Majumdar cites the DLF Cup played in Kuala Lumpur, Malaysia in September 2006 as an example of cricket played for satellite television. Majumdar questions the reason behind three of the world's top teams (Australia, India, and the West Indies) travelling to a country where cricket is not very popular to play each other. He writes:

Why was the BCCI desperate to send the Indian team to play before a paltry crowd of 7,000 Indian expatriates? Even with temporary stands, erected specially for the purposes of the DLF cup, the Kinara Oval in Pouchong, Kuala Lumpur could only house just over 7,000 spectators. Further, why did the BCCI spend $4 million to install floodlights at the venue when any stadium in the Indian heartland or in any of India's North Eastern states would have been far better off with such an installation? Was it simply to improve the viewing for the 7,000 odd? Finally, was such a huge outlay for such a small audience justified? Or was there yet another ulterior motive that went far beyond the politically correct argument of trying to boost cricket in Malaysia and thus furthering the timeless objective of trying to globalize cricket?[41]

Majumdar conjectures that the primary reason behind such a series was 'nothing more than attractive programming organized for the Indian satellite television market by the BCCI'. He quotes Nalin Mehta, who claims that 'by 2006, cricket-oriented programming accounted for the greatest expenditure in news gathering across most news channels'. He seems to suggest that television in India is highly dependent on cricket for both viewers and revenue. He even goes as far as to say that Indian television has been subject to 'cricketization'. The game of cricket itself is highly suitable to television viewing, providing, as it does, a lot of time during play in which no action that influences the outcome of the match takes place on the field—such as while changing ends at the end of an over and the drinks break to name a couple—providing advertisers ample time to promote their products.

It has been argued that what one watches on television is a whole other event as compared to the game that is witnessed in the stadium. According to Sut Jhally, 'television does not present us with a sports event but with a sports event (already highly structured by the commodity logic) that is mediated by television'.[42] Some of the highest-rated non-sport programmes on television in the few years preceding the birth of the IPL were reality shows—The Apprentice, Big Brother, American Idol (and their regional counterparts), to name a few. In a Packer-like move, in order to attract those viewers who do not watch cricket as a matter of routine and those whose interest in one-day cricket had dwindled, the 'think tanks' of television and cricket together came up with a format of cricket that would last as long as a movie, and would still be called cricket—Twenty20.

Conclusion

All of these changes in cricket have stemmed from reasons other than the actual game of cricket itself. These changes have influenced and changed the game profoundly; not just in the way that it is played and judged, but in every aspect of engagement—from stadium spectators to television viewers, and from the reporting of cricket in print and electronic media to the range of professions that now exist within the game. It is almost as if the core of the cricket world has shifted from the actual game and is no longer assembled around one single and identifiable centre that dictates the direction of the evolution of the game. The birth of Twenty20 cricket is but one more non-linear point of evolution in this multi-centred, multi-faceted industry of cricket.

The central technological device in the game of cricket, and indeed all sport, is the television. Not only is the game played mainly for televised broadcast, but it is also the primary means of revenue for most sporting bodies and even sportspersons whose endorsement deals involve monetizable television appearances. Chapter 3 will attempt to unpack the intricacies of televised sport and its implications for sport and sportspersons.

3

What's All Your Furniture Pointed At?

Late in the ninth season of the American sitcom *Friends* (2002–2003),[1] the eponymous friends find themselves at a Palaeontology conference in Barbados, where Ross Geller—the 'geek' in the gang—is the keynote speaker. As he enters the conference venue with Joey Tribbiani—the star of the hit daily soap opera *Days of Our Lives* in the show's universe—a delegate approaches Ross and asks for an autograph. Delighted to be recognized and appreciated, he introduces his friend, Joey who the lady appears to not know. In an effort to jog her memory, Joey—sure of his celebrity status—tells her that she probably recognizes him from 'a little show called the *Days of Our Lives*' and flashes his celebrity smile at her. 'I'm sorry, I don't own a TV', she tells him. Incredulous at this revelation, Joey asks, 'you don't own a TV?! What's all your furniture pointed at?!'

Revealed in the punch line is a tacit acknowledgement of the ubiquity of the TV set—known to us variously as the telly, the idiot box, or the small screen—and the influence it has on our everyday lives. Aldous Huxley, in *Brave New World* (1932), foresaw our present with an eerie clarity when he wrote of a hospice in the future where at the foot of every bed was a TV,[2] 'Television was left on, a running tap, from morning till night'. It has now become a most integral part of all our lives.

From news and current affairs to gossip and voyeurism, from drama and fiction to music and science, and from cooking and travel to sports and war, the television screen (or versions of it on various devices) is the thing we turn to for almost all our information and entertainment needs. Unlike the computer and the internet, in which data transfer can be two-way, the television is a machine that merely relays. The most control a user has is in switching to different broadcasts. The TV will brook no discussion, allow no dissent, and entertain no protest.

Sports and television, of course, have now become completely inseparable; so much so that televising of sport has become the central

Speeding up Sport. Vidya Subramanian, Oxford University Press. © Oxford University Press 2022.
DOI: 10.1093/oso/9780192865120.003.0004

reason for a sports event—cricket or otherwise. The Olympics are a case in point. As Amit Gupta has pointed out, even a sporting event of the stature and scale of the Olympics is only considered a 'commercial success' when it is held in 'a time zone that is friendly to western television audiences'.[3] The implication is that unless there are enough people who will watch an event on television, it can no longer be considered a success.

In India, this trend is visible in the manner in which domestic cricket matches, that were once a thriving site of fan attention, now go almost completely unwatched. In an article in *The Hindu Business Line*, Vijay Lokapally reflects on how even though some of the biggest names in cricket in India (and indeed the world) play in these matches, stadium audiences are all but non-existent.[4] He cites examples of Ranji matches and even domestic T20 matches that are not part of the televised spectacle that the Indian Premier League (IPL) is. This is not just a feature of domestic cricket in India or the subcontinent. The story is much the same in County Cricket matches in England. ' "Two men and a dog" is how English cricket writers often sum up the audience on the county circuit', says Lokapally.

While some observers credit this diminishing crowd interest to the decreasing quality of domestic cricket, it is clear that unless audiences can be engaged via televised entertainment packages, the sport in the stadium is not a draw. And the lack of enthusiasm for even domestic Twenty20 leagues (not counting the IPL) suggests that it has nothing to do with the length or format of the game. The article cites the example of a 2014 North Zone Twenty20 league match in which fan favourites Gautam Gambhir and Virender Sehwag were playing, that had practically no stadium audience.

In an interview, G. Rajaraman,[5] a senior sports communication professional and Founder Editor of Horizon Sports Pvt Ltd., directed my attention to the several television screens at the restaurant we were at (three out of the four that we could see were showing sports. One showed cricket and the other two football—it was during the FIFA World Cup of 2014) and pointed out to me what was in his opinion, 'a much better way to see the game'. Why would one take the trouble to get to the stadium, put up with uncomfortable seats, terrible toilets, and endless security restrictions to watch a match, when you can get not only much better quality but also get to see more famous players on the TV—in HD, no less, he argued. 'We no longer watch cricket', he said, 'We are watching cricketers'.

Platforms and Pedestals

The medium of television is one that is highly suitable for the making of stars and individual celebrities. In the words of Gary Whannel, 'The close-up-centred basis of television helped transform sports performers into stars and celebrities. Televised sport made top performers recognizable stars, enhancing their earning potential from endorsements and advertising'.[6] The televised sport is not just a sport. It has become, among other things, 'a branch of the advertising and promotion industry'.

So much so that when Indian captain Mahendra Singh Dhoni suddenly announced his retirement from Test cricket at the end of the third and penultimate test in the India-Australia test series in December 2014, speculation centred as much around his brand value as it did around the reasons for such a sudden decision. At the time, Dhoni was endorsing more than twenty brands, earning upto INR 13 crores (almost USD 2 million) per annum per project. His 'brand value' was speculated to be USD 20 million.[7] Advertising and marketing gurus commented that Dhoni's 'brand' was in no danger of declining because of his retirement from Test cricket. The article quotes Prahlad Kakkar as having said that 'Dhoni's brand value was not because of Test matches, it was because of ODIs and T20. So as long he is playing, he should be fine'. Another advertising professional, Prasoon Joshi is quoted to have said, 'there is a different dimension (that has been) added to the personality. Every stage of the career brings in different dimensions and attributes. It is not just about cricket for him. He is seen as a story whose life is good enough for a book or a film ... Every step somebody takes will change the way the brand is consumed. In his case whether it will take a turn for good or worse it remains to be seen'.

In an online article titled '50 Most Marketable 2013'[8] the writers detail the criteria for the list: 'the central criteria that shaped the list were value for money, age, home market, charisma, willingness to be marketed and crossover appeal'. The only male cricketer on the list in 2013 was Virat Kohli at Number 13. Dhoni, while missing from the 'most marketable' list, made it to the 'most marketed' list[9]. Ellyse Perry, the Australian woman who has represented her country in both football and cricket, is the only other representative of cricket on the list. In the 2014 version of the same list,[10] Perry was no longer on it and Kohli had moved up to

Number 2. Given the limited number of countries that play cricket, this would have been surprising. But as the writers explain, 'no sport, anywhere, holds as big a market as India in such thrall'.

More surprising was the inclusion of Kevin Pietersen, former English captain who was forcibly retired by the England and Wales Cricket Board (ECB) in February 2014. Without a national side to play for, Pietersen's entire marketing portfolio (when the article was written) was based on his association with the IPL and other Twenty20 tournaments that do not require to co-ordinate with the ECB. Pieterson's marketability appeared to be independent of his career in the national side. Since having left the English side, he had written a book,[11] been in several advertising campaigns, captained the Delhi Daredevils in the IPL, played in the Caribbean Premier League for St Lucia Zouks, played in the Big Bash League for the Melbourne Stars, been on the BBC's Test Match Special commentary team for the 2015 World Cup in Australia and New Zealand,[12] and made a viral spoof video of Ashes 2015 predictions, complete with self-deprecating humour about his own absence from the English side.[13]

It becoming increasingly clear that sport and indeed sportspersons are all part of a larger structure of buying and selling. A question to consider at this point is who is the seller? And who is the buyer? While it seems as though the 'things' that are being sold are the goods advertised during the telecast of a sports event, there do seem to be wheels within wheels. As Gideon Haigh points out, it is Cricket Boards (especially the BCCI, 'the biggest and the meanest representative' of all Cricket Boards) that do most of the selling. He writes of the 'seminal shift in the relations of administrators to the administrated, from one in which boards held the game in trust on behalf of their public, to one in which they seek to own the game and sell it to "cricket consumers" '[14]; which then transforms (what was traditionally known as) a fan into a buyer, a consumer. It is a clear change in the way that cricket, and indeed all sport was once engaged with—what was once merely enjoyed, is now also 'consumed'.

Azhar Habib[15], owner of ICC's broadcast partner Wild Track productions, explained the buying and selling to me. 'The [broadcast] rights of any series lie with the host board', he told me:

> ... If an India Pakistan match is happening in Pakistan, Pakistan Cricket Board would own the rights. India would also get some money out of

it, but they're owned by the host boards. And then each host board has their own arrangement in terms of broadcast. They have their rights cycle ... 4 years, 6 years, 7 years, etc. So they would sell their rights internationally, and any broadcaster can buy the rights. [A broadcaster] can buy worldwide [rights] or they can buy a certain territory and then sell it to various other territories.

[For instance], Star bought the worldwide rights for ICC events. So, around the world Star owns the rights and then Star further licenses it to broadcasters around the world. Star has a marketing team and a licensing team which sells these rights around the world. So if Star gives a guarantee money of, say, a billion dollars to [the] ICC, then it is up to them how they raise that one billion dollars. So, from India they might raise 900 million. And the remaining money they might want to recover from various other territories. So they'll sell the rights to a Sky Sports in the UK, Fox in the US, Fox in Australia, Super Sport in South Africa, PTV in Pakistan ... and say, '50 million dollars, next seven years, all ICC cricket on Sky Sports in the UK'. So, that 50 million is going to come to Star Sports, not to ICC. Because Star has already bought the worldwide rights

Advertising time is then sold by these broadcasters to companies that wish to 'buy' airtime to 'sell' their products on air. The audiences are then 'consuming' both the sport and the advertisements.

Kerry Packer was the first to transform the cricket fan into a consumer. His World Series Cricket (WSC) was the first cricket tournament to bring in the sort of razzmatazz to cricket that we have now come to accept as *de rigueur*. In spite of having been disparagingly called a 'flying circus', the WSC changed the way cricket was seen and enjoyed forever.

The 'Circus'

In the words of Osman Samiuddin, 'Without changing the sport too much, Kerry Packer changed the game completely'.[16] And indeed, he did. He was the first to see the massive potential of television for cricket, or to put it another way, the massive potential of cricket for television. A keen businessman and one of the first people to recognize the impact and reach of television, Packer figured out in the 1970s that a new and potentially massive audience awaited cricket on the other side of the TV set, and cricket could now be 'sold' to this audience, making the sport more lucrative than ever before. It was with this idea in mind that the Australian newspaper magnate and owner of the Channel Nine network managed to successfully negotiate exclusive broadcast rights to the Ashes in 1977 with the English Test and County Cricket Board (TCCB). Having experienced the audience enthusiasm of the Ashes on TV, Packer made a bid to the Australian Cricket Board (ACB) for exclusive Television rights for the next three years.[17] But while the ACB was willing to concede commercial rights, it wasn't willing to take away broadcast rights from the Australian Broadcasting Corporation (ABC), with whom, according to Martin Williamson, the ACB shared 'a long-standing, and some said far too cosy, relationship'.[18]

Miffed at this refusal, Packer masterminded an event that, while not very successful in its first outing, would change the way cricket was seen, played, enjoyed, and understood. Knowing that in comparison to other sportspersons, cricketers were abysmally underpaid, especially in Australia, Packer enlisted several Australian cricketers who were drawn to the lure of his venture. He was planning a rival cricket league in secrecy, backed by his considerable corporate wealth. Later at a press conference, he would say that cricket was the easiest sport in the world to take over, because nobody had bothered to pay the players what they were worth.[19] With the help of English captain Tony Greig as his agent, Packer managed to sign several top English players, and Asif Iqbal brought in some 'important Pakistanis'. The readiness of the West Indian team that came *en masse* and the willingness of the South Africans who hadn't played international cricket in several years made what was initially supposed to be merely an Australia versus the Rest of the World programme into a full-fledged international series—World Series Cricket (WSC)— complete with large-scale logistics and massive financing. The story of Packer's clash with the establishment is well documented and more popular for the telling.

The ICC didn't take the Packer series too seriously at first, because it seemed at the time to be a largely domestic problem in Australia. But as it became apparent that several reputed cricketers of all nations had signed on for the WSC, the ICC decided to meet with Packer to try and negotiate a truce—an attempt that failed when Packer insisted that exclusive TV rights for the 1978–79 season be awarded to Channel Nine. Since this was outside the ICC's jurisdiction, no agreement could be reached, and the ICC announced that no matches organized by Packer would be admitted as first class and any cricketer playing for his series would be banned from first-class and Test cricket. Responding to this slight, Packer, in the words of Williamson, 'launched his lawyers' against the ICC and other national boards when Tony Greig, John Snow, and Mike Proctor sued the TCCB claiming 'restraint of trade'. The plaintiffs won the case and were awarded costs to the tune of £200,000. In spite of the win in court, Packer could not use the term 'test match' or even call the team 'Australia'.

This led to the coining of the term 'Supertest' and the team was called 'WSC Australia XI'. The other two teams were the 'WSC World XI' and the 'WSC West Indies XI'. The problems for WSC were by no means over, though. Not having any cricket grounds to play matches on, Packer would have to lease non-cricket stadia in major cities for matches. He accomplished this in collaboration with his groundsman John Maley by devising a hitherto unheard of concept of drop-in pitches. These were pitches that were grown in greenhouses and brought to the stadium.

After pulling through the legal hassles and the logistical problems, Packer, with the likes of Richie Benaud, Gary Sobers, Bob Cowper, and Ian Chappell on his team, launched the WSC in 1977 with very little initial success. Commenting on the debacle, *Wisden* quotes Packer as having said, 'We are still amateurs, but we are more professional than we were, and will become even more professional'.[20] This setback propelled Packer to inject into the second season the technological gimmicks, the razzle-dazzle, and all kinds of fanfare that are today part and parcel of cricket.[21] Describing this phenomenon, a disparaging Tony Lewis in the *Sunday Telegraph* in January 1979 called the WSC 'Kerry Packer's Flying Circus'.[22]

Selling Sport: Expanding the Horizon

That was the first time that cricket was 'sold' to the public the way it was. The WSC was never just cricket. It was a whole other 'product'. With a blitzkrieg (for those days) of off-field publicity, Packer was making sure that players were projected as stars; as Ayaz Memon put it, 'caricatured and then sold to a public looking to satiate vicarious curiosity and desires

as stereotypes'.[23] According to *Wisden*, Packer had always claimed that
the reason the first season of WSC was a disappointment was mainly because 'people had been so heavily indoctrinated against the idea'. His response to that was to try and indoctrinate people to pick his new idea
over the idea of traditional cricket.

To this end, Packer ensured that as many Australian newspapers as
possible had a former player (who was on the Packer payroll) 'banging the
drum'. Packer used his own television network to reinforce the publicity
he was generating in other spaces. That was not all. Along with coloured
clothes for players (a first for cricket) and matches under floodlights (another first) with an easier-to-spot white ball, Packer, as Lalit Modi would
do several years later, was selling not cricket, but entertainment. *Wisden*
described it thus:

> Packer gave the public free parking at Sydney, free transport out to the
> Waverley ground in Melbourne, and played his matches when spec-
> tators have time to watch—at night, and with a white ball which they
> can see better. In addition, with his television network, he promoted his
> stars as Hollywood used to theirs in the thirties. They became house-
> hold names and faces. It was all a personality cult.[24]

Ayaz Memon agrees with the description of the 'personality cult', empha-
sizing that it was 'nurtured and developed assiduously through television
sports shows, or radio interviews or even live appearances at local markets and shopping centres'. Along with promoting cricketers as celebrities,
the WSC injected the game with technology in an attempt to make it as
different as possible from traditional cricket. One of Packer's great ideas
was cameras on both ends of the pitch. Until then, every other over was
seen from behind the wicketkeeper. Packer apparently told his production team, 'Who wants to watch a batsman's bum for half the match?'[25]
Playing under lights was another one of the several shots of adrenaline
that cricket received through the WSC.

Catering to audiences at home in front of their TV sets and to spectators in the stadium, both of whom could now watch cricket after their
workday was over, Packer added what today could be called *bling* to a
game that once was played in white flannels for five days with a stiff upper
lip. He was attempting to woo what Memon calls 'the peripheral, the

non-traditional cricket fan'. The publicity slogan for night matches was 'Big Boys Play at Night' and it became 'more than just an innuendo' when Playboy bunnies rode out in flashy cars on to the field to serve refreshments during the drinks break.[26] A move mirrored in the IPL's inclusion of cheerleaders for their matches.

The marketing was specifically aimed at acquiring more and more eyeballs for the game. This would ensure a larger audience, which could then result in larger revenues, by providing advertisers with a deeper reach. Women and children—not the primary target of cricket so far— became central to Packer's marketing. The personality cult and the selling of cricketers as icons and personalities were targeted at getting more women interested in watching cricket, if not for the sport, for the players. The novelty of the night matches, the strategic placement of cricketers as brands, and his ability to work the press all resulted in the recruitment of new audiences for the game, and more importantly, for the advertisers and funders.

After a successful tour of West Indies in 1978–79, based on Packer's ability to bring the West Indies Board out of the financial instability it was in then, it was becoming increasingly clear that the powers that be were willing to accept that this new format could co-exist with the old form of cricket. In the words of *Wisden*, 'It was not a pie in the sky that would go as it came, simply because of the established business principle that he could now negotiate from strength'.

Even though the series in West Indies was marred by instances of crowd violence and the infamous incident of Ian Chappell being charged, convicted, and fined in a Georgetown magistrate's court for assaulting a local WSC official and using indecent language, the series was financially a success. 'Whether the product is good, bad or indifferent, much of its success or failure lies in marketing techniques, and in this respect Packer has clearly shown the way to success', observed *Wisden*. Following the series, in April 1979, the Australian Cricket Board finally granted Packer what he had originally wanted: exclusive television rights to test and other matches in Australia for Channel Nine. And with that, from January 1980, the WSC was disbanded. In three years, Packer had taken the game and changed it irreversibly. In the words of Greg Manning in *Wisden* Australia, 'Packer didn't spend $12 million buying the game; he spent $12 million turning it into something that could be bought'.[27]

Once the cricketing establishment wizened up to the immense monetary potential that one-day cricket held, it did not take long for the ICC to incorporate many aspects of Packer's WSC into the mainstream of cricket. The number of one-day fixtures organized by the ICC went up, and with the doors having been flung open for corporate money to enter cricket, cricket was being transformed from being just a game to becoming a platform for the promotion of the wares of the sponsors. Several commentators have spoken of this change in cricket having been inevitable, but it would not be too far-fetched to conjecture that but for the vision of some individuals (particularly Kerry Packer), it is very likely that cricket could have taken a very different shape. In its transformation from being a game without speed to becoming a successful advertising platform, something fundamental in the soul of cricket had changed.

Sport: A New Platform

The influx of corporate funding and advertising into mainstream sports allowed sporting fixtures, games, uniforms, and even stadia to become advertising billboards. This led to a direct increase in the amount of money within the administration of cricket, which then found its way on to the field by way of increased monetary compensation for cricketers, the influx of support staff for teams and individual players, and the use of more and, as some would argue, 'better' technology in the game.

But the most important of these influxes has been the television. The platform that cricket has become has been constructed on the foundation of television, even if it is assembled by bringing together several other, sometimes even unrelated building blocks. The immense profitability of modern-day cricket comes from its highly lucrative position as an immeasurably useful platform. No longer just a game, cricket has become the kind of platform that can provide more 'eyeballs' than any other marketing gimmick.[28]

Consider the example of India Cements. Owners of the Chennai Super Kings (CSK) franchise, India Cements was among the least known franchise owners when the IPL began in 2007 (the company has been described as being 'perceived to be a conservative, publicity-shy, and provincial operator') and therefore most in need of an advertising fillip.

Having *bought* Indian one-day captain Mahendra Singh Dhoni (the most *expensive* player in the first edition of the IPL at $1.5 million), India Cements was all set to use their IPL team as a high-profile 'calling card'.[29] N. Srinivasan, Vice-Chairman and Managing Director of India Cements, is quoted to have said,

> Even if the company had spent Rs. 1500 crore on brand promotion, it wouldn't have got a fraction of the publicity that Super Kings got us. The team's brand equity will help expand our business in north India. We have big plans to be a pan-India corporate group.

Piggybacking on the popularity of the team, India Cements planned to launch an all-India cement brand, Super Kings, packaged in the instantly recognizable yellow of the team jerseys. Alam Srinivas and TR Vivek have pointed to another and highly visible example of IPL as a marketing vehicle. Vijay Mallya, 'whose personal PR humbles that of Sir Richard Branson and Donald Trump', they say, was clear from the outset that his team—Royal Challengers Bangalore (RCB)—was a platform to promote his other business interests such as his airlines and his liquor brands, 'which he couldn't advertise through conventional media because of government restrictions'.

Advertising even made it into the commentary box in the IPL. Writing of commentators becoming part of the advertising world, Osman Samiuddin comments on their use of brand names of companies *sponsoring* sixes, fours, and other moments, 'Each six was a "DLF maximum", each critical point in the game a "Citi moment of success"... This was commentary as PR'.[30] Almost every aspect of the game, from the field to the commentary box, had been appropriated in the assembly of the platform.

The Player as Canvas

The sportsperson too has been co-opted into the canvas of advertising and branding. Says G. Rajaraman, 'there are ten properties on the player, including the cap'. Translated, this means that there are, on average, ten spaces for logos, branding, and advertisements on the person of a player at any time. The IPL's 'Clothing and Equipment Regulations' in 2014 listed in detail the manner and form of logos and advertisements allowed on a player's person. 'Diagram A' of the regulations document showed the list of 'properties' on a player's uniform.

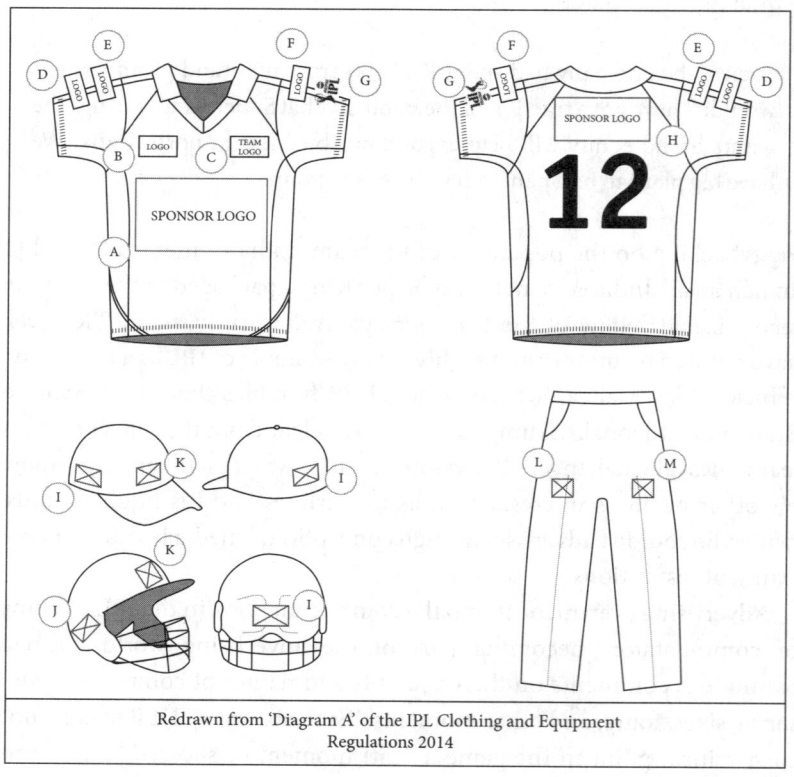

Redrawn from 'Diagram A' of the IPL Clothing and Equipment Regulations 2014

Position A—Main logo on front of shirt
Position B—Upper right logo on front of shirt
Position C—Team logo on upper left front of shirt
Position D—Lower logo on non-leading arm
Position E—Upper logo on non-leading arm
Position F—Upper logo on leading arm
Position G—Pepsi IPL competition logo on lower leading arm
Position H—Upper back logo of shirt
Position I—Rear logo on headwear
Position J—Leading side logo on headwear

Position K—Team logo on front of headwear
Position L—Right logo on trousers
Position M—Left logo on trousers

Out of the thirteen listed positions, three (C, G, and K) are either the IPL logo or the Team logo. The other ten are for sponsors and other logos—six on the playing shirt (or sweater), two on the trousers, and two on the headwear (helmet, baseball cap, or sunhat). Each position is priced differently, such as a logo on the leading arm of a player would, understandably, be worth more than that on the non-leading arm, owing to greater visibility to the television cameras. The 61-point document[31] that covers everything from the colours to the sizes of logos to be used in kits for teams and players (including those for non-playing members and what players should wear for practice, for matches, and for even media interviews) makes for fascinating reading. Detailed descriptions were provided for everything from the bibs that non-players should be wearing to the allowed colours of players' caps and even undershirts, such as:.

Article 6: 'Undergarments (worn under playing shirt) shall be of the same colour as the predominant colour (the "base colour") of the playing shirt or colour of the sleeve. Plain white undergarments may be worn provided they do not protrude from the sleeves'

Article 15 (Caps and Sunhats):

15.1: 'The colours and design of caps and sunhats shall be uniform to all members of the same team save for those who wear the orange and purple caps. The holder of the orange or purple cap must wear the cap whilst fielding'.

15.2: 'Franchises are permitted to have a player's order of representation number on the non-leading side of the playing headwear. For example, a player could be the 25th player to represent a franchise and would therefore be permitted to have "25" written on the playing headwear. The number must be written in the alinea font and its height must not exceed 2 cm. This number may be different from the player number on the back of the playing shirt'

While the IPL logo and team logos are of an exact specified size at specified locations, the regulations leave the room (at the 'sole discretion' of the BCCI) for commercial logos to change and alter during the course of the tournament. Conflicts of interest between sponsors of different teams are allowed, but not with those of the host team.

> **Article 23:** 'Both teams shall abide by any law of the host venue, which restricts advertising of a product. No compensation shall be payable should a team be precluded from displaying its commercial logos on clothing or cricket equipment, and a visiting team shall not pursue any action against the BCCI, host franchise or state association'

Bats, pads, socks, shoes, and most other equipment are also allowed to have manufacturer/sponsor logos. The canvas for advertising in an IPL match (as indeed in international matches) is as intricate as it is vast—encompassing players, stadia, broadcast channels, and even the commentary. It is not just players who serve as billboards, it is the commentators and umpires as well. Each slot is numbered, priced, and sold, making ad revenue the lifeblood of the enterprise.

The ICC too has regulations for clothing and equipment (downloadable from the ICC website) that also contains detailed rules about the size and number of logos and manufacturer's identity markers on clothing and equipment including stumps (no regulations on colour; event logo or logo of the series or sponsor may be displayed on each stump) and socks (one manufacturer's logo on each sock). The document covers clothing for test matches, One Dayers, and Twenty20 matches held under the auspices of the ICC (events like the IPL, the Big Bash League, and Champions league T20 are independent of the ICC).

Not only is this is a far cry from the white flannel cricket that was once the only cricket seen but it is also a big step forward from the coloured clothing that was introduced in the Packer era. The inclusion of the player in branding opportunities on the field also brings with it a different set of conflicts such as the one about ambush marketing—players not wanting to be seen around prominent logos of brands that are in direct competition to those that they personally endorse. In the months leading up to the World Cup in 2003, much was written about the inability of players to sign contracts with the ICC due to conflicts with personal endorsements. In the 1996 World Cup, for instance, Sachin Tendulkar—one of several Indian players who were signed up by Pepsi—would not even be seen near the drinks cart and would have the 12th man bring him drinks because the cart was built to resemble a large Coca-Cola bottle; Coca-Cola being the official sponsor of the World Cup.[32]

Building Brands

But branding opportunities in sport are not just for manufacturers and sponsors. A successful player is himself (and in cricket, it has usually been a 'him') a brand. The price he commands for an advertisement spot or a public appearance stems directly from his performance and reputation as a cricketer. India's most successful cricket captain Mahendra Singh Dhoni could command a price as high as some major film stars for an ad spot. It speaks to the 'saleability' and 'dependability' of a player in the eyes of the audience.

So much so that in 2013, in the wake of the much publicized spot-fixing scandal, when N. Srinivasan, the then President of the BCCI and owner of the Chennai Super Kings (CSK) IPL franchise had to step down, he insisted that his detractors were 'jealous' of him because he 'had Dhoni'. 'Why do you think people are jealous of CSK?' he is reported to have asked,[33] 'It is because of Dhoni. There was a savage attack on me because I have Dhoni'. He was referring to allegations of impropriety after the arrest of his son-in-law Gurunath Meiyappan in the same scandal. 'Having' Dhoni is more than just about 'owning' the captain of the Indian team. Apart from playing for the team in corporate tournaments organized by the BCCI, Dhoni's success as captain is a useful marketing tool in the arsenal of the company he represented as Vice President (India Cements). For someone who began as a ticket examiner for the Indian Railways, MS Dhoni's rise has been appropriately described as 'meteoric'. Before his turn with India Cements, he had also been an employee of Air India. He was even given a promotion after India's World Cup victory in 2011. Dhoni, along with Yuvraj Singh, Suresh Raina, and Harbhajan Singh were all members of Air India staff, where they represented Air India in corporate tournaments.[34] Other prominent employees of India

Cements were all-time great Rahul Dravid, spin bowler R. Ashwin, and wicketkeeper–batsman Dinesh Karthik.[35]

Making the IPL

In an interview I conducted with Hemant Buch, Vice President of Production at *Ten Sports*, he described in detail the process of putting together a live telecast of a cricket match. Speaking of a fixture in the Caribbean, he speaks of heading a 'smaller set-up' of about 35 to 40 people. 'In the IPL, you'd have about 80 people', he tells me. Showing me an image of a complicated console that looks more like a spaceship navigation system out of a science fiction fantasy movie, he points to his 'Programme Monitor' and the 'Preview Monitor'. Along with a colleague who pushes buttons to instantly relay the shot that he wants to be relayed, Buch is the Director of the match, and it is his job, as he sees it, 'to tell the story to the audience'.

On average, he tells me, an international one-day match would have 10 manned cameras and about 10 to 12 unmanned ones. Depending upon needs and budgets, this number can go up to 13 or very rarely even 17 manned cameras. Azhar Habib, of Wild Track Productions pegged the number of cameras in a single IPL match at about 30 to 34. The fixed cameras, such as the Mat Camera, the Run-out Cameras, and the Beauty Camera don't require to be manned since they have been fixed to record from the same angle continuously. Others such as the Follow Camera are the ones that need to be manually handled. The Follow Camera is, as the name suggests, the one that follows the ball from the moment the batsman hits it to wherever it finally goes.

Once the batsman makes the shot, the two follow cameras on either side of the pitch follow the ball as it either reaches a fielder or makes it to the boundary and beyond. Other cameras such as the Spider Camera are remotely manned. The Spider Camera is a roving camera that moves above the playing field and captures images from a bird's eye view. A team of about 500 people work on the production of the match in the broadcast team alone. Each stadium is 'rigged' with what Habib calls, 'kilometres and kilometres of cabling' and other attending equipment such as the cameras, the slow-motion machines, replay machines, audio systems, etc. up to two days before match day. Including the pre- and post-match shows that are now an inextricable part of the televised sports experience, a single one-day international is a massive affair by any yardstick. The IPL is, if anything, larger than regular one-day series, and while match times may be shorter, the complications of broadcast only go up.

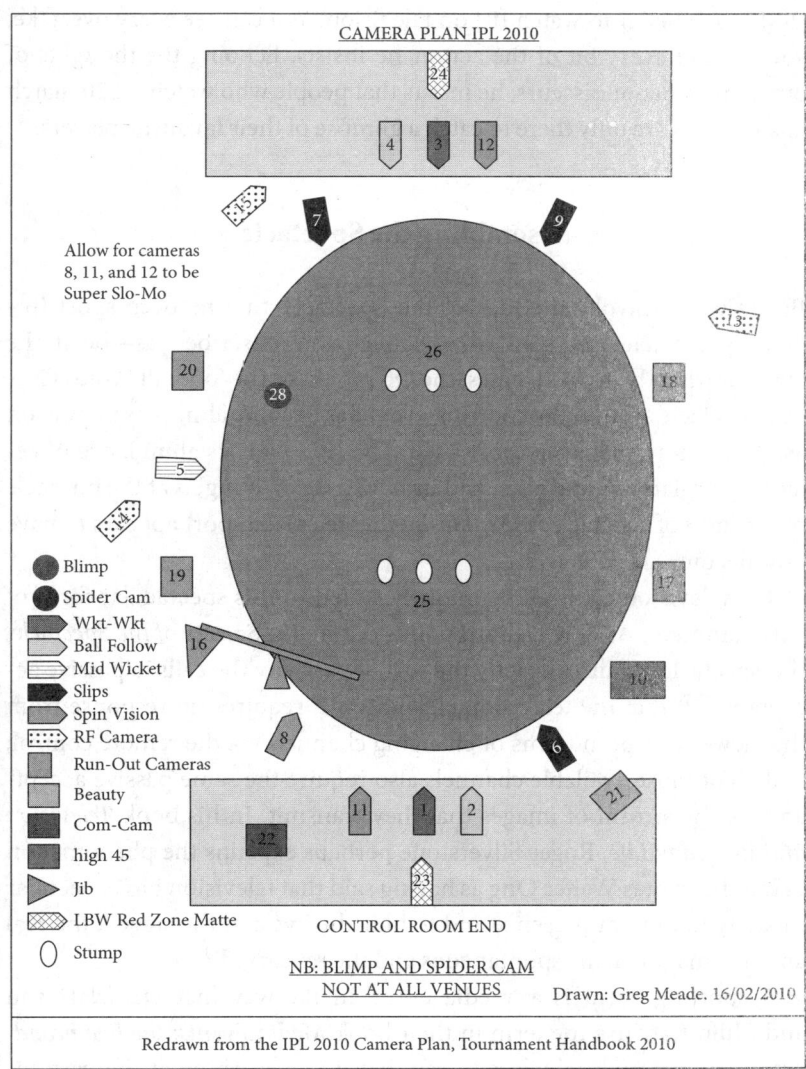

CAMERA PLAN IPL 2010

Allow for cameras 8, 11, and 12 to be Super Slo-Mo

Blimp
Spider Cam
Wkt-Wkt
Ball Follow
Mid Wicket
Slips
Spin Vision
RF Camera
Run-Out Cameras
Beauty
Com-Cam
high 45
Jib
LBW Red Zone Matte
Stump

CONTROL ROOM END

NB: BLIMP AND SPIDER CAM
NOT AT ALL VENUES

Drawn: Greg Meade. 16/02/2010

Redrawn from the IPL 2010 Camera Plan, Tournament Handbook 2010

Speaking of the pace at which the IPL and now other domestic T20 tournaments such as the Big Bash League are played and televised, Hemant Buch equates IPL style T20 matches with Formula One, questioning the wisdom of watching the game in a stadium at all. 'what is there to watch in Formula One?' he asks. 'For me, it's just cars going round and round. You can't see the whole circuit ... you can't see what is happening. [It's] much better to watch [it] on television. You can see every overtake, you can see every bit of the action' he insists. Echoing the thoughts of other cricket connoisseurs, he insists that people who watch a T20 match in a stadium are only there to catch a glimpse of their favourite players.

Assembling the Spectacle

Buch's words invoke the idea of the 'spectacle' that modern sport (especially the televised kind) has come to be described as—be it the Superbowl in the United States, the Olympics, or the football World Cup. The spectacle around the sporting event has become almost as important as, if not more than, the sport itself. The IPL, with its abundance of celebrity, its glamour and glitz, and its blitzkrieg of 'bling', is at the pinnacle of the kind of spectacle, the *tamasha* that televised sport appears to have now become.

The television set itself is uniquely suited to this spectacular form of entertainment. As Guy Debord points out in *The Society of the Spectacle*, the 'spectacle' requires exactly the sort of passivity (he calls it 'passive acceptance'[36]) that the television engenders. It requires no response from the viewer except in terms of changing channels via the remote control; and all of those available channels also require the same passive acceptance of the stream of images that they transmit. In his book *Television and Everyday Life*, Roger Silverstone perhaps explains the phenomenon best as he quotes Walter Ong as having said that television has a 'peculiar capacity to present presence and to blur the live and the staged, the real and the imagined, the spontaneous and the rehearsed'.[37]

A sporting event is a 'media event' in the way that Daniel Dayan and Elihu Katz use the term in their book *Media Events: the live broadcasting of history*,[38] which is to say that it is happening at the very instant of watching it on television, and is necessarily an 'interruption' of a schedule, much like 'holidays that halt everyday routines'. The 'live' nature of the broadcast ('the French call this *en direct*') makes it necessarily unpredictable, and consequently exciting. Typically, Dayan and Katz point out, such media events are '*organised outside the media* and ... at least theoretically, the media only provide a channel for their transmission. By "outside" we mean both that the events take place outside the studio in what broadcasters call "remote locations" and that the event is not usually initiated by the broadcasting organisations'.

This is, theoretically, true of all sports broadcasts today. The event itself is not initiated or organized by the media that broadcast it; however, it is the broadcast and its attending frills that are the main drivers behind the organization of the event—be it the World Cup of football or cricket, the Olympics, or even the IPL. The television companies that broadcast the event are not its organizers but have *bought* from the Sporting Bodies (FIFA, ICC, BCCI, etc.) that organize the event the right to broadcast it and earn revenue from it. Before television became the primary mode of engagement with sport and sporting events, the event was news, and the media played the role of what has been called 'a witness' to the event. When radio and television first began reporting and broadcasting cricket, says Gideon Haigh, it was with a 'sense of privilege and deference. They were honoured guests in the house of sport and remained low-key, polite'.[39] He contrasts this with the scenario today in which 'the media runs cricket, (and it has been realized) that cricket owes everything to its electronic availability'. He goes on to say that, 'The media now fancy they are entitled to be their own spectacle, to draw attention to their presence rather than remain silent witnesses'. The broadcast—which automatically means televised broadcast, it now seems, is the reason for the event and not vice versa.

Dayan and Katz theorize that the 'festive viewing of television' (in terms of events that are televised as they occur and 'transfix a nation or the world' such as the Olympics, a royal wedding, etc.) can be easily classified into three categories: 'contests, conquests, and coronations'. All of these telecasts, they argue, are recognized by audiences as 'an invitation—even a command—to stop their daily routines and join in a holiday experience'. The reality, they maintain, is uprooted by media events. The space within which the *live* event is occurring becomes, for the time of the broadcast, 'only a studio'. They go on to say,

Thus conquering space in an even more fundamental way, television causes events to move off the ground and 'into the air'. The era of television events, therefore, may be not only one in which the reproduction is as important as the original, as Benjamin (Walter Benjamin in 1968) proposed, but also one in which the reproduction is more important than the original.

This appears to echo the thoughts of Debord in *The Society of the Spectacle* in which he suggests that the spectacle has become the centre of all life, and meaning that was once derived from *being* and was 'obvious(ly) downgraded' into *having* due to the 'economy's domination of social life', has now further shifted from *having* to *appearing*. He writes, 'The present stage, in which social life is completely taken over by the accumulated products of the economy, entails a generalized shift from having to appearing: all effective "having" must now derive both its immediate prestige and its ultimate *raison d'etre* from appearances'.[40] A statement that eerily foreshadows the present age of social networking, in which even personal life events are measured by the number of 'like's on a post.

It is then not surprising that the primary way in which the popularity of IPL teams and their 'fan engagement' is analysed is through social networking sites such as Facebook and Twitter. The number of tweets per match and the number of retweets and 'followers' is today one of the more accepted metrics that advertisers and organizers depend on to gauge the level of fan commitment and interaction.

Networked Media Sport

'Television is dead. Long live television' begins the book *Sport Beyond Television: The Internet, Digital Media and the Rise of Networked Media Sport* by Brett Hutchins and David Rowe.[41] The message is clear. While the televised version is still the primary way in which sport is viewed, it is not necessarily through the TV set in the living room. If *Friends* had lasted another decade, Joey Tribbiani might have been surprised to find that a lot of furniture no longer faces that particular technological contraption.

In fact, media events today are rarely, if ever, planned without a comprehensive strategy for online distribution and broadcast. With the advent of streaming services and better broadband internet speeds, the distinction between online viewing and viewing sport on the TV set is blurring. As, Hutchins and Rowe put it, 'While broadcast television is still a prime attraction for audiences ... (there is) evidence of a rich and popular second screen experience for fans and viewers, with mobile phones and devices evidence of a third screen'. They refer to this 'appearance and operation of media sport in the digital age' as 'networked media sport'. This analysis, while acknowledging the changes to televised broadcast sport, considers all screens of viewing still a television phenomenon. This is reasonable since most online or mobile phone viewing is almost exactly the same as the televised content. While experiments with differing camera angles and other add-ons for online viewing are being tried out, largely the viewing experience remains the same, with the added dimension of viewer comments, 'like's and sharing possibilities through social media.

The IPL too is available for viewing on second as well as third screens. In 2010, in what was referred to as a 'path-breaking partnership with Google', the IPL broadcast stream was made available online through the video streaming behemoth YouTube.[42] The IPL Tournament Handbook describes it as 'This revolutionary tie-up puts the fan in the driver seat— s/he can now decide when to watch games, irrespective of broadcast timings. All games will be available online and accessible at all times, giving the fan the freedom to create his/her own schedule'. In the 2015 edition, all matches of the IPL were available for live streaming on Hotstar. This move was, in a way, revolutionary; because traditionally (or what stands for tradition in the fast-paced, ever-changing ICT-enabled media landscape), online viewing had always been seen as a threat to the broadcast televised presence of sport. The open and networked mode of functioning in an online universe has always been viewed as a threat to the 'closed, centrally controlled models of content production and distribution characteristic of the analogue-broadcast era'.[43] It is estimated that in 2010, the IPL-Google tie-up carried the IPL live to about 50 million viewers, and also attracted several high-profile advertisers such as Hewlett-Packard and Coca-Cola.

In conclusion, it would be fair to surmise that sport—a highly perishable commodity—is first, a media event, and second, a televised event. The 'networked media sport' landscape provides a suitable substrate for the development and perpetuation of events such as the IPL, giving advertisers and audiences alike a relatively new consumption pattern, that can be moulded to enhance individual celebrity, brand identification, advertising revenues, and indeed the visibility of high-profile sports and sportspersons.

It is important to note that the entire Networked Media Sport economy exists for one specific entity—the fan, the spectator, the audience. An important question that then arises here is who the people for whom this entire edifice exists are. The shaping of the platform and the creation of such a spectacle are based on an understanding of what 'fans' or 'spectators' seemingly desire. The following chapter will attempt to understand the construction of the spectator for whom the sporting-entertainment complex has been so carefully constructed.

4

The Eye of the Storm

P.G. Wodehouse, in one of his comic masterpieces, *The Mating Season*, places his blundering protagonist Bertie Wooster in a crowd at a village carnival where his friend Esmond Haddock has just performed a rendition of a hunting song. The performance that follows Haddock's, the audience finds, leaves something to be desired. At a pause in action on stage, writes Wodehouse, in his inimitable style[1]:

> 'We want Haddock,' he said. 'We want Haddock, we want Haddock, we want Haddock, we want HADDOCK!'
>
> He uttered the words in a loud, clear, penetrating voice, not unlike that of a costermonger informing the public that he has blood oranges for sale, and the sentiment expressed evidently chimed in with the views of those standing near him. It was not long before perhaps twenty or more discriminating concert-goers were also chanting:
>
> 'We want Haddock, we want Haddock, we want Haddock, we want Haddock, we want HADDOCK!'
>
> And it just shows you how catching this sort of thing is. It wasn't more than about five seconds later that I heard another voice intoning.
>
> 'We want Haddock, we want Haddock, we want Haddock, we want Haddock, we want HADDOCK!' and discovered with a mild surprise that it was mine. And as the remainder of the standees, some thirty in number, also adopted the slogan, this made us unanimous.

It is an easy illustration of the effect that runs through crowds, and how one single sentiment becomes the voice of a mass of people. As Gustave LeBon pointed out in *The Crowd: A Study of the Popular Mind* in 1895, a 'psychological crowd' is a 'provisional being' created in certain moments and made up of 'heterogeneous elements, which for a moment are combined' to produce, he suggests, a being different from each individual

Speeding up Sport. Vidya Subramanian, Oxford University Press. © Oxford University Press 2022.
DOI: 10.1093/oso/9780192865120.003.0005

that forms it. He compares it to a living body that is comprised of several wholly different cells that come together to form the organism.[2] A crowd is not formed by the accidental accumulation of human beings in any particular place 'without any determined object'; he posits,

> To acquire the special characteristics of such a crowd, the influence is necessary of certain predisposing causes ... Thousands of isolated individuals may acquire at certain moments, and under the influence of certain violent emotions—such, for example, as a great national event— the characteristics of a psychological crowd.

The crowd that watches a spectacle and demands to be entertained is what advertisers want to be seen by. It is for this crowd that the spectacle exists and takes the form that it does.

The crowd, then, is the thing that exists at the core of all spectacle. The crowd, the viewers, the audience is the reason there is theatre and cinema and art and indeed, sporting events. The Indian Premier League (IPL) is one of these massive, audience-heavy events, making it an effective platform for seekers of publicity. As advertisers and publicists have discovered, the sporting arena is one of the most effective ways of 'grabbing eyeballs' in the modern world. The spectacle of sport—be it individual sports like tennis, or team sports like football, or even endurance sports like the Tour de France—are all much loved and much-viewed spectacles that make them excellent platforms for those seeking to be seen. Piggybacking on the popularity of the spectacle, in exchange for financial support to organizers, players and the sport, advertisers have managed to successfully convert the sporting 'arena' into a 'platform'.

Who Are the Watchers

This makes an interesting site at which to enter the question of who it is that the advertisers seek to be seen by; and for whom the platform is constructed. The crowd at Bertie Wooster's village carnival is quite different from the 'crowd' (if it can even be called that) at a modern sporting event. The chief 'audience' of a sporting event is, curiously, absent from the site of the spectacle. The manner in which an event, sporting or otherwise, is broadcast 'live' to millions of people around the world, changes the notion of the 'crowd' that exists at the heart of a spectacle. The 'crowd' now is all of those people watching the show on television, on the internet, and in public spaces, all put together. They may be sitting with friends, family, or alone, but have become part of the spectating 'crowd'. This fragmented, non-unified, and yet seemingly all-powerful 'crowd' belongs to what French theorist Paul Virilio has called the 'city of the instant'. This 'city' is a virtual space in which almost everyone, everywhere in the world can be watching an event 'live' on screens—on computers, televisions, mobile phones—even if it is separately and individually.

Steve Redhead, in 2007, quotes Virilio from an interview in the early 1980s as having said, 'those absent from the stadium are always right'.[3] For it is those that watch the spectacle of the event on television and the internet for who the event is, he argues, 'produced'. Virilio said,

> The billion people who watch the Olympic Games in Moscow, or the soccer championship in Argentina, impose their power at the expense of those present, who are already superfluous. The latter are practically no more than bodies filling the stadium so that it won't look empty. But their physical presence is completely alienated by the absence of the television viewer, and that's what interests me in this situation. Once, the stadiums were full. It was a magnificent popular explosion. There were 200,000 people in the grandstands, singing and shouting. It was a vision from an ancient society, from the agora, from paganism. Now when you watch the Olympics or the soccer championship on television, you notice there aren't that many people. And even they, in a certain way, aren't the ones who make the World Cup. The ones who make the World Cup are the radios and televisions that buy and—by favouring a billion and a half television viewers—'produce' the championship. Those absent from the stadium are always right, economically and massively. They have the power. The participants are always wrong.[4]

Further, Redhead argues that 'the stadium is effectively transformed into a television set'. He goes on to write of the curious manner in which fans in the present day watch the sport. Spectators at home watching the sport on their screens are essentially, Redhead asserts, 'treated to the spectacle of spectators within the grounds, watching not only the replays of incidents on giant screens but also the game live on screens on their mobile phones'. So they are, in effect, watching people watch the event. Even those present at the stadium end up watching the game and replays, etc. on the giant screens within the stadium. Thus the entire 'watching' experience of the sport appears to have become mediated through various screens—whether at home on the television, in the stadium on the giant screens, or even on mobile phone screens anywhere in the world.

A sport played by the British elite, taking five days to play out a single game, often a draw with no winners or losers, cricket was a unique and leisurely sport. Today, cricket in India is as much a sport as it is entertainment. When our team is winning, the players are Gods, but when they are not, their homes and family may be pelted with stones. This sort of extreme reaction from fans is not uncommon and elevating certain cricketers to the status of 'God' is fairly usual. 'Cricket is our religion and Sachin is our God' is one of the most recognizable phrases in the several hagiographies that one can find floating around of the admittedly incredible batsman Sachin Tendulkar.[5] In 2015, there were more than five television channels in India dedicated entirely to cricket that telecast cricket-related content twenty-four hours a day, seven days a week. And the IPL—a relatively new version of the game—is one of the most popular televised sporting events in the country. Many fans I spoke to seem to believe that even though cricket may have originated in Britain, its spiritual home is now in India. Played everywhere from *maidans* to narrow streets, cricket is as ubiquitous in India as that other national pastime—Bollywood.

Alongside this seemingly passionate adoration of the sport and its practitioners, however, there exist many observers who feel that there is a lack of any technical, in-depth engagement with the nuances of the game. One television sports producer that I interviewed was of the opinion that present-day fans of cricket in India care only about the glitz and glamour surrounding the game, understanding only the easy binary of win-loss; and do not really care about or understand the nuance and technique that makes cricket such a unique sport in the world. He went as far as to call all the hoopla surrounding the IPL a *tamasha*.

Writing on memory and forgetting in Indian cricket, Satadru Sen[6] attempts to explain this proclivity of modern-day Indian fans of cricket. The word *tamasha* (meaning 'carnival') pops up in his work too, and he suggests that more of cricket than just the playing 'field' has begun to come into focus since Kerry Packer revolutionized the game with his World Series Cricket (WSC). Sen seems to be implying that as more of the off-field happenings in the cricket world such as the birth of the 'celebrity cricketer' (that brings to mind one of the first of that ilk—Imran Khan in his famous 'Big boys play at night' T-shirt) and the treatment of cricketing heroes like those of the movies made it easier for the non-connoisseur to engage with cricket. This 'gossipy, personality-driven' and glamorous mode of engagement with cricket, he suggests, led to a 'democratisation of the culture of sport in India—that is, its emergence from the confines of the field and the world of male experts'. Together with economic liberalization, increasing spending power, and the emergence of cable TV in India, 'a flush new market' for cricket was made available.

Spectators, Crowd, and the 'Post-Fandom'

The spectator now engaged with the sport in new and hitherto unseen ways. The expert connoisseur gave way to the boisterous fan who just watched matches in which India played hoping for victory and to enjoy the carnival that cricket became precisely in order to attract this kind of audience. Writes Sen, 'Those who participate in online polls on "Will India win the World Cup?" or "Should Ganguly be sacked as captain?" probably do not assume that the question poses a worthwhile intellectual challenge or requires a deep technical knowledge of the game'. This new fan—one that seeks to merely enjoy the moment of the match—is perhaps what Steve Redhead refers to as a 'post-fandom' where fans as consumers use sport to promote themselves as 'cool' instead of other motivations such as national or regional identity, etc.[7]

Focussing on football, Richard Giulianotti, theorizes that the 'hypercommodification' of football has led to a change in the manner of engagement of the spectator with the sport and the club. He categorizes the football spectator (a sport that is primarily played by small, local clubs) into four types: supporters, followers, fans, and flâneurs.[8] Giulianotti's analysis posits that there are four 'ideal-type categories', into which spectators can be classified. Since the analysis is based on spectators of football in Europe, which is dominated by a deeply entrenched club culture and in which local club affiliations are potent cultural identifiers, the categories cannot be adapted directly to fit cricket and the IPL. However, the categorization merits analysis and provides a useful lens through which to view the fandom of cricket in general, and the IPL in particular.

Studies of the commodification of football that took place in the 1960s and 1970s suggest three distinct categories of spectators: members, customers, and consumers—they categorize the football fan. 'Members' were those who saw themselves as a part of the club; 'an identity rooted in the unbreakable reciprocal relationship between fan and club'. The 'customer' was seen as one with more fluid loyalty, a relationship based on 'the satisfaction of public wants' where if these wants were not met adequately, the 'customer' could take his emotional investment elsewhere. The third category of 'consumer' is one that has 'no brand loyalty but is instead a sporting variant of economic man, an exemplar of rational choice'. The consumer spectator is seen as being highly likely to switch support from one club to another based on winning teams or those 'which are more socially suited to advancing the spectator's social and economic mobility'.

Giulianotti argues that while those three categories may be a good starting point to understand the fandom, the 'hypercommodification' that football has seen deserves a different classification; one based on 'the particular kind of identification that spectators have toward specific clubs'. He charts four categories as being underpinned by two basic binary oppositions: 'hot-cool' and 'traditional-consumer' (Figure 4.1).

The horizontal traditional/consumer axis has been set up to measure 'the basis of the individual's investment in a specific club: Traditional spectators will have a longer, more local and popular cultural identification with the club, whereas consumer fans will have a more market-centred relationship to the club'. The vertical hot-cool axis has been set up to reflect 'the different degrees to which the club is central to the individual's project of self-formation. Hot forms of loyalty emphasize intense kinds of identification and solidarity with the club; cool forms denote the reverse.

The traditional/hot spectator here is defined as a 'supporter' of the football club, who has a 'topophillic'* relationship with the club. For such

---

* According to Giulianotti, 'topophilia involves an intense emotional attachment to a particular part of the material environment; otherwise stated, it is a love of place'.

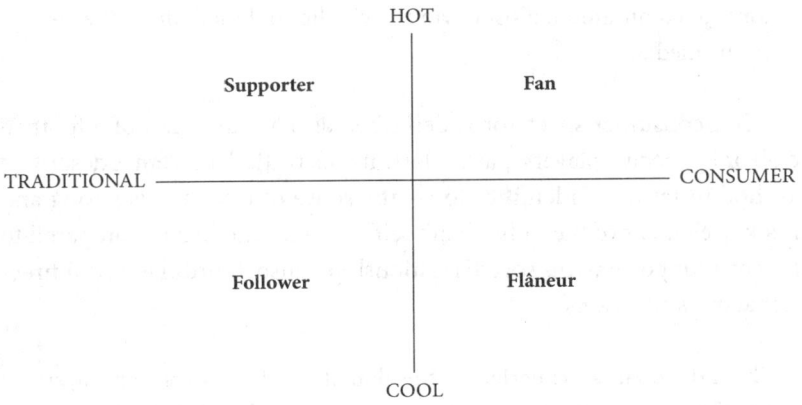

Figure 4.1 Redrawn from Richard Giulianotti's classification of spectators
Source: Richard Giulianotti. 'Supporters, Followers, Fans, and Flâneurs: A Taxonomy of Spectator Identities in Football', *Journal of Sport & Social Issues*, 26, no. 1 (February 2002), p. 31.

supporters, 'subcultural capital' cannot be acquired by simply purchasing club commodities. These are spectators that have an intimate relationship with the club, and consider themselves 'members' of the club and as having a stake in it. Giulianotti writes,

> The classic supporter has a long-term personal and emotional investment in the club. This may be supplemented (but never supplanted) by a market-centered investment, such as buying shares in the club or expensive club merchandise, but the rationale for that outlay is still underpinned by a conscious commitment to show thick personal solidarity and offer monetary support toward the club.

The traditional/cool spectator is classified as a 'follower', not just of the club but also of 'players, managers, and other football people'. The follower keeps abreast of developments in the club and other football people he is interested in. According to Giulianotti,

> The follower has implicit awareness of, or an explicit preconcern with, the particular senses of identity and community that relate to specific clubs, to specific nations, and to their associated supporter groups. But the follower arrives at such identification through a vicarious

form of communion, most obviously via the cool medium of the electronic media.

The hot/consumer spectator is described as a 'modern fan of a football club or its specific players, particularly its celebrities'. This fan is described as 'hot' in terms of identification—'the sense of intimacy is strong and is a key element of the individual's self'—but is still distant compared to that of a supporter. This sort of relationship is also 'inordinately unidirectional in its affections'.

> The individual fan experiences the club, its traditions, its star players, and fellow supporters through a market-centred set of relationships. The fans' strength of identification with the club and its players is thus authenticated most readily through the consumption of related products.

Since the fan primarily engages with the club through market-centred relationships, this makes these fans of football rather similar to fans of leading musicians, actors, or media personalities. All of these relationships are 'largely unidirectional' in terms of identification. Thus this sort of fandom can only exist for large, wealthy clubs. Giulianotti theorizes that 'the brand loyalty and inelastic demand of fans for club shares and merchandise' are actually constructed by the clubs themselves in order to provide the club financial stability. But promoting a transformation of supporters into fans makes it easier for fans to drift to other 'markets (other leisure activities, other football leagues, though probably not supporting rival teams) in the deculturalized pursuit of "value for money."'

Since fan identity is based on a 'unilateral' relationship that is fundamentally different from one that arises out of face-to-face interaction (as is possible with supporters), Giulianotti posits that, 'such a relationship is dependent on specific media that allow for a continuous and multifarious flow of star-related signs toward the fan'. He goes on to say that, 'these more shallow, mediated forms of acting help to preserve the highly profitable, parallel football universe that has been constructed to supply the fan market'.

The last category of cool/consumer leads directly from the above and can perhaps be seen as further down the spectrum from the fan. This category—that of a flâneur—is that of the 'unreconstructed cool consumer'. As Giulianotti writes, 'The flâneur acquires a postmodern spectator identity through a depersonalized set of market-dominated virtual relationships, particularly interactions with the cool media of television and the internet'. A category more carefully understood by Walter Benjamin, a flâneur is typically described as usually male, adult, bourgeois, 'an idler and a traveller', 'an urban stroller ... (who) would promenade through boulevards and markets'. Drawing on that, Giulianotti writes,

> The flâneur ... consumes these signifiers in a disposable and cliché-like fashion, as if adopting a temporary tattoo. Moreover, the football flâneur's natural habitat is increasingly the virtual arena, seeking the sensations of football as represented through television, internet, or perhaps in the future, the audiovisual bodysuit. Thus, television presentation of football is tailored toward a flâneur-type experience. Television compresses time-space differences, distilling entire matches or tournaments into 100-second transmissions of blinding, aestheticized action, to an accompanying backbeat that drifts between techno and opera.

Flâneurs are expected to be able to switch connections with teams or players, and even relinquish the game (football) in favour of other forms of entertainment. They have no topophilic identification with the club, and are 'emptied of any sense of home, but house instead the cool and ungrounded circulation of football's commodity ephemera'.

While club cricket is (and indeed has always been) a thriving sport, it is not the most popular form of the game. Corporate tournaments and other city and club level tournaments exist, and have their share of fans and following, but the larger and more popular forms have always been state- or country-level competitions, such as Ranji Trophy, Duleep Trophy matches in India, or county cricket in England, and the international competition, which climbs to its pinnacle during the World Cup once every four years.

Be that as it may, Giulianotti's analysis and classification provide a useful taxonomy through which to view the spectators of cricket as well. I argue that the 'supporter' category cannot be directly transposed to cricket because it doesn't apply to either the national form of the game or even to the new IPL club form of the game. While club loyalty at a local level exists, it cannot be compared to the football fandom in which 'members' buy season tickets to watch all the games of the favoured club at the home ground, and a reciprocal relationship of membership to the club drives an emotional investment in it.

The categories of 'follower' and 'fan' could perhaps be collapsed into one single category in terms of fans of cricket, particularly in India, since the fandom is largely unidirectional, without the teams actually considering fans 'members' of the administrative or emotional core of the team organization, be it at a state or national level. The 'spatial embedding' and topophilia of the 'member'; the engagement with the sport and teams through the 'cool medium of electronic media' of the 'follower'; and the strong sense of intimacy that the 'fan' feels for his or her team are all markers of the traditional Indian cricket fan. There has been, largely, only one team that most traditional Indian cricket fans have rooted for—the national team—and their loyalty is both passionate and topophilic, and also primarily engaged with through various 'cool forms' of media.

The identity of the 'flâneur' though, is one that is easily identifiable as that of the target demographic of the IPL. Subject to what Giulianotti calls 'the growing commodification of social relationships and objects', the IPL fan's social practices, in keeping with Benjamin's definition, are oriented more towards consumption than a deeper engagement with the sport. The television presentation of football, maintains Giulianotti, is 'tailored toward a flâneur type experience'. This is true for the IPL as well. The description of flâneurs as 'window shoppers' too can be easily transposed to fans of the IPL, who are also 'motivated to seek sensation, excitement, and thus to switch their gaze across clubs, players, and nations'. IPL then, as Giulianotti suggests, 'encourages the germination of a proxy form of narcissistic self-identity for the cool consumers'.

New Roles for Spectators

In 2009, former West Indian batting great Brian Lara, while calling cricket a 'dying sport' and 'welcoming' the new Twenty20 form of the game, suggested that this new format brings to the sport a whole new kind of spectator: 'ones that just want to go to the game and don't even know what happens'.[9] He appears to suggest that the draw of cricket, and indeed the IPL is not the game of cricket itself but all the razzmatazz attached to the televised version of the sport. The lack of knowledge about the longer version of the game or the nuances and intensity of the sport doesn't seem to bother the fans of this new age spectacle. The aforementioned sports director expressed a similar opinion. Having directed live cricket over a long period of time and having watched the evolution of television in sport telecast in India, he believed that the fans of cricket in India today are not interested in the sport itself. He cited an example of travelling with some cricket fans on a train in England a few years ago who were discussing the batting technique of a batsman in great detail, and contrasted that with fans in India now whom he felt were only interested in the 'tamasha' in sports.

In contrast to that position, some fans of the sport have argued (to me in informal settings) that the television and all its attending frills have created a more engaged audience than ever before. They reasoned that the add-ons to the game, such as super-slow-motion replays and ultra motion cameras, make this generation of fans the most knowledgeable of all the ones that came before. The argument is a viable one. The great number of available technologies within broadcast that seem to be making television viewing 'better than ever before' are a great way of learning and engaging more deeply with the sport. With analysis of games with experts that go on for hours (in two languages, now—English and Hindi) before and after the match, it would be unsurprising to find better-informed viewers and more engaged fans. But is it really making the viewer experience 'better' and 'more enriching'? If television ratings, the amount of cricket programming on air at any given time, and the almost unbelievable amounts of money spent on acquiring television rights are any indication, then the answer must be in the affirmative, these fans argued.

On the contrary, I believe that these very markers may denote a different phenomenon. The large amount of television viewership, the massive amounts of money invested in broadcast rights, and the unceasing coverage of cricket on sports channels indicate (probably) an increase in the number of people watching cricket, but there is no way to know whether these are informed fans of cricket seeking to fruitfully engage with the game in new and 'better' ways; or simply watching the event for its entertainment value.

One of the issues raised before the IPL was created was how the viewership for cricket on TV was dwindling. According to Rohit Gupta, President of Sony Entertainment Television, television ratings for one-day matches had tapered off from above ten in 2003 to almost three in 2008.[†] 'It clearly showed that viewers didn't have the eight hours to watch an ODI (One Day International). It meant that youngsters were moving away from cricket, forget about adding new consumers', he says.[10] It was at this juncture that Lalit Modi took the cricket world and the Indian entertainment world by storm and created the IPL.

Importing the idea of privately owned franchises from a combination of football's EPL (English Premier League) and the American NFL (National Football League), Modi created a television-centric, cash-rich, celebrity-driven, non-national, cricket-based product that he went on to sell to the world. With a format borrowed from English football, a power centre in India, television programming structured on the lines of America's NFL, and with players from cricket playing countries all over the world, the IPL was a truly globalized event.

Set up as a response to the ICL (Indian Cricket League) that was created by Subhash Chandra of the Zee Network in a move mirroring Kerry Packer's (both Chandra and Packer created separate cricket leagues after being refused television rights by their respective National Boards),[11] the IPL was as much like the WSC as it was not. Sensing a challenge from the ICL and rushing to reach the profits before Chandra, the BCCI responded with its own cricket league—the IPL—and imposed a ban on the rival league. With corporate owners of franchises, player *auctions*, cheerleaders at every game, and programming schedules for almost all games to be played at night to ensure maximum viewership, this was a version of cricket that had its centre in business acumen and free-market philosophies than in the game of cricket. Liquor barons, movie stars, large real estate developers, media management firms: everyone was invited.

[†] TRP or Television Rating Point is the viewership rating for any broadcast programme over a period of 30 days. TRPs quantify the gross rated points achieved by the broadcast among targeted individuals within a larger population.

The IPL was targeted not at the traditional cricket fan, but at everyone who had an interest in television, in cinema, in celebrities, particularly the young, upwardly mobile city dwellers. Television commentator Harsha Bhogle attributes the birth of the IPL to the need for cricket to keep the attention of youngsters who were now more inclined to watch football. The attempt, once again, seems to be to lure the spectator in the periphery.[12] 'Cricket was desperately in need of fresh ideas because at least in the big metros, it was losing kids to EPL. Children had begun to think of cricket as the dad's game' he is quoted to have said.[13]

David Rowe and Callum Gilmour describe the IPL as a 'strange hybrid of the English village green, "Bollywood", and the Super Bowl'. They also echo the voices of Redhead and Virilio when they describe the modern sport as a 'mediated "live" cultural form in which the in-stadium crowd is a key part of the spectacle'.[14] Rowe and Gilmour quote Andrew Wildblood, a senior employee of the global sports marketing and management firm IMG that helped prepare a blueprint for the league, to have said that the IPL was intended to cater to the expanding leisure and entertainment economy. Lalit Modi admitted as much in 2008 when he said,

> We are not pitching IPL against cricket; we are pitching it against the prime time (7 to 11 p.m.) of general entertainment channels ... To make a show a hit, one needs star attraction. We have cherry picked the best players from across the world ... We have added a lot of music to the games. I think it provides entertainment to the crowds and between breaks. People are able to lap it up and enjoy it—it's an evening out, A Bollywood movie is three hours. This is a three-hour function. A lot of good food and catering and popcorn and ice cream for the kids.[15]

It would appear that in place of creating a more discerning fan, new cricket is more about finding new and more entertainable audiences through the game of cricket, not just those who don't have the patience for a day-long game (far less a five day one) but also those who may only be interested in the allied industries of celebrity and entertainment.

With a package that boasts of Bollywood stars, industrialists and their celebrity scions, and cricketing celebrities from around the world, the IPL is a crucial moment in the understanding of sport and television in present-day India. Targeted for television audiences, rivalling the general entertainment channels, built around individual celebrity, and used as a platform for large corporate firms and film stars alike, this new form of cricket has reshaped the idea of sports television in India.

Bringing technology such as the intrusive spider camera (which was famously shooed away by Sachin Tendulkar in IPL 2011[16]), Mongoose bats, and interviews of players while they are playing on the field, the new Twenty20 version of cricket has brought into the game more technology than ever before. All this seems to have altered the manner in which cricket as a game was imagined in the minds of the players, the administrators, and those who follow it. All the technologies, the marketing strategies, and the corporate backing together seem to have re-assembled the brass tacks of cricket to create a structure that is now a strong and powerful platform for the promotion of everything from fast-moving consumer goods to individual celebrity brands and large corporate identities.

This is the age of 'instant' everything. Cricket writer Ivo Tennant speaks of the modern viewer's need for the 'gratification of the ball flying over the boundary rather than studying the immaculate Boycottesque defence of the craftsman'. He bemoans the loss of 'Messrs Craft and Guile' in the Twenty20 framework, calling it a game for 'the modern, fidgety, fast-evolving society in which concentration levels are miniscule'.[17] The trappings and the suits, as it were, of the televised spectacle are then but attempts to keep this 'fidgety' viewer from reaching for the remote. Out of the several millions that watch cricket, the percentage of the engaged connoisseur remains miniscule, believes a senior television professional who agreed to speak candidly off the record. He called not just the IPL but also all of the present-day cricket programming in India a *tamasha*.

Transcending National Boundaries

Unlike other club-based sports, cricket was always primarily a game played by nations; or in domestic games, states and counties. Fans picked allegiances based on the happy accidents of geography, and tournaments were organized around geographic boundaries. On the surface of it, the IPL is a fundamental reworking of that notion. With city-based clubs competing for the top spot, the fan base could be expected to be localized around the cities and stadiums used as 'home grounds'; perhaps envisioning in the long run spectators who will become 'members' as Giulianotti defines them in terms of football fandom.[18] But since the IPL is primarily a televised spectacle, the fans of the tournament do not end up coalescing around the local cricket ground or cities. In interviews conducted in several public places in Delhi between 2013 and 2015, I found that most respondents did not name the local team—Delhi Daredevils—among their favourite teams.

On further questioning, several respondents answered that it was because the team was one of the most unsuccessful ones in the league. Several others named their favourite players as reasons for picking other teams (such as M.S. Dhoni for Chennai Super Kings, Yuvraj Singh and Chris Gayle for the Royal Challengers Bangalore in 2014, etc.). This was somewhat different for IPL fans in Chennai, many of whom seemed to revel in the fact that the team named for their city was so successful, and it appeared to have come together into a sort of brand identity of their city that is different from the 'madrasi' descriptor that they are usually assigned.

Another criterion for fans picking 'favourite' teams seemed to be the fame of actor Shah Rukh Khan. Several fans picked the Kolkata Knight Riders because of its association with the movie star, in spite of them (or him) having no association with the city of Kolkata. Several respondents (mostly female, who admitted to not being interested in cricket at all) knew not only which team the superstar owned but were able to correctly identify almost all teams in which movie stars held a stake—such as Priety Zinta's Kings XI Punjab and Shilpa Shetty's Rajasthan Royals.

However, it was also clear that the main loyalty of the fans surveyed was first to the national team. The World Cup is considered the most important cricketing event and beating Pakistan is the most 'satisfying victory'. Patriotic identity associated with the national cricket team provides a sense of pride in its victories and collective shame in its losses. It is not a large leap to conjecture that it is this deep emotional investment in the fortunes of the national team that emerges as the public outpouring of joy at India's victories and a violent backlash against the players after losses. It isn't just the team of eleven men who win or lose. It is 'we won' or 'we lost'.

The IPL is attempting to harness that same emotional appeal of India's winning by creating a league in which no matter which teams played, won, or lost, India never lost. Or to put it in the words of Gideon Haigh,[19] 'India always wins'. Haigh's theory was that it was the aftermath of the 2007 World Cup that gave a fillip to the setting up of the IPL. This World Cup, held in West Indies, in which both India and Pakistan had been knocked out in the league stages, has been widely reported to have been a financial disaster.[20] This was because there was a major drop in interest in the subcontinent once the two teams were knocked out, and most of the advertising revenue for cricket matches comes from the subcontinent, and especially when India is playing. This led to the reworking of the World Cup format to ensure that the 'best' teams stayed in the fray as long as possible.

Recovering from a humiliating exit from the 2007 World Cup, Lalit Modi and the BCCI pitched the IPL. In the words of Gideon Haigh, 'So, Lalit Modi went around in the wake of the 2007 World Cup and said, "Okay Indian corporates and Indian broadcasters, that was really bad; but I'll tell you what I've got. I've got a tournament in which India always wins. And Indian participation is guaranteed all the way through." That's the essence of the IPL'. Set up to lure disappointed Indian broadcasters, corporate advertisers, and Indian spectators back to cricket; the IPL brought the best international talent from around the world to play for local teams, and created a spectacle that was to be played and contested within India, but looked and felt every bit as international as the World Cup. And the underlying theme of the entire enterprise would be that no matter who won and who lost, the famously mercurial Indian spectators would always have an Indian victory to celebrate. That the first edition of the IPL in 2008 came soon after India's victory in the inaugural T20 World Cup in South Africa in September 2007 was an added boost.

Much of sports sociological theory is in agreement that sport is able to whip up national frenzy just like war, and events like the Olympics serve to consolidate the feeling of 'playing for one's country' or 'doing it for the motherland'. Scholars such as Chris Schilling and Philip Mellor have even written on reconceptualizing sport as a religious phenomenon in the modern era.[21] They argue that the old tropes of focussing on sport as a religious or quasi-religious phenomenon do not adequately explain the sentiment attached to the sport, and it thus requires an understanding that embraces both secular and religious phenomena.

Comparing sport with war, Amarnath Amarasingam has noted that, 'international sporting events like cricket serve not only as a form of national recreation, but also national re-creation[22]'. He quotes Rob Nixon as having said that sporting events are 'exhibitionist events imbued with the authority to recreate or simulate the nation, offering a vigorous display of a proxy body politic'. The IPL too, I argue, is a part of this project.

In an online survey I conducted, several respondents in talking of the IPL expressed a positive sentiment regarding the manner in which the league allowed Indian players to closely interact with the best international talent. The IPL was, they seemed to suggest, an excellent place for Indian players to better their skills and learn from the international players participating in the league. In spite of the corruption scandals, the over-the-top frenzy, the cheerleaders, and the famous IPL parties that seemed to draw forth a negative response, there appeared to be a wide positive reaction to the Indian players playing alongside and learning from international talent and making India look good in international competitions.

That nationalism is one of the IPL's important central themes is also made evident in the highlighting of the country in the advertising campaigns for the league. The 2015 edition of the IPL that came hot on the heels of the World Cup, was advertised as '*yeh hai India ka tyohar*' ('This is the festival of India'), making it abundantly clear that the emphasis was still on the country as an emotional resonating point with the target audience. Fan identity in the IPL, after more than a decade of existence, has not organically developed around the geography of the teams in the league. This is in spite of the vigorous social media campaigns that IPL teams set up. Taglines that obviously aim to imbue a local flavour in fan engagement such as the use of a Tamil slogan in the hashtag '#WhistlePodu' (blow a whistle) for the Chennai Super Kings; or the extensive ad campaign worded in simple Punjabi for the Delhi Daredevils—'*Dilli ke apne munde*' or 'Delhi's own boys'—have failed to elicit the kind of local fervour that the marketing teams had perhaps hoped for.

That is not to say that there is no following at all, given the several internet forums, Facebook pages, and blogs that seem to overflow with fan loyalty to one or another IPL team or player; but this outpouring of sentiment does not appear to be either widespread or in any way city or region based. An interesting point to flag here would be that large parts of India remain unrepresented in the yearly gala that is the IPL. At one point, the state of Maharashtra had two teams in the league—Pune Warriors India and Mumbai Indians—while large and populous states like Madhya Pradesh, Uttar Pradesh, etc. had no teams at all.

In some editions of the IPL, several teams switched or added an extra 'home ground' on which to play. Kings XI Punjab played no matches at the picturesque Dharamsala ground in 2015 and moved instead to Pune, while the Delhi Daredevils added Ranchi as a second 'home ground' (in 2013, Ranchi was the second 'home ground' for the Kolkata Knight Riders). Some of this has been attributed to financial concerns regarding gate money and other revenue sources. The Pune ground has a larger number of corporate boxes as compared to Mohali or Dharamsala, and since it has hosted IPL matches in the past, it was considered an adequate addition (or replacement) for the Kings XI team.[23] It seems like a tall order then, to expect the people of Pune, Maharashtra—be they follower-fans or flâneurs—to embrace a team called 'Kings XI Punjab' as their home team and to identify with the team simply based on the venue of their new home ground. The Delhi Daredevils and Kolkata Knight Riders may have brought the IPL to Ranchi (home of Indian captain M.S. Dhoni and site of one of the BCCI's new stadia), but to expect any sort of fan loyalty for either team from the people of the city might perhaps be asking for too much.

It is thus my contention that the main motivation for spectators who follow the IPL is still the consideration of the country above all else. To be able to watch current and future stars of the Indian team play explosive cricket; and to be able to see international fan favourites play alongside Indian superstar cricketers is still the thrill of the IPL, almost a decade and a half after the idea was first executed.

Reshaping Spectators

With the advent of this 'city-based cricket'[24] in which loyalties are divided between cities, players, and even owners of franchises (as has been seen in the IPL), the identity of the cricket fan has become almost indefinable. Writes Srinivasan Ramani,

In the past, Indian cricket was used as a tool to buttress nationalism; and the Indian cricket team was meant to represent the Indian nation in international competition. The players in the national team were therefore performing a national duty.[25]

But the fans now pick their teams on no definite criteria, changing the way cricket has hitherto been engaged with. Ramani writes of the influence of corporate interests in the game, which has caused players to become 'commodities' that can be bought and sold in an auction, the corporates to become 'owners' of these players, and the 'value of the commodity is determined by a set of rules that play themselves out on a *maidan* with cricketing instruments and more so on the television screen in the form of commercials'

Teams no longer represent a nation or even (such as in the Ranji Trophy) regions or states. Teams and players have been *bought* and their allegiance lies foremost to their team owners. Players are no longer playing for a passionate cause such as the nation. Even national teams are known (on Twitter at least) as the Boards that run them. The official Twitter handle of the International Cricket Council (ICC), while tweeting about a test match between England and India in 2014 said, '@ECB_Cricket has the best of Day One of the Fifth Test, dismissing @BCCI for just 148 before finishing 62/0 #EngvInd'.[26] While it is clear that this was merely a way to identify the teams and tag the respective Boards' Twitter handles, the identification of the team as the Board that runs it seems to hit a familiar nerve. It is a sentiment reflected in the opinions of some former fans of cricket as well. In 2014, I met several former cricket followers who were vocal about their mistrust of the Cricket Boards that 'run cricket'. 'I refuse to call this team the Indian team', one respondent said, 'they should be known as the "BCCI Eleven" because they are administrated by a private entity'.

I engaged in an informal conversation with this set of former cricket enthusiasts—all professionals between the ages of 25 and 35—who watched cricket with enthusiasm through their school years and now follow football with much of the same zeal. During the course of this conversation, it emerged that their interest in cricket had begun to dwindle around the same time that the match-fixing scandal of 2000[27] broke and football (in the form of the English Premier League) began to be televised in India in 2001.[28] Having switched allegiances almost entirely to football now (so much so that while speaking about football, they refer to the team they support as 'we'), these city-bred professionals are cynical about cricket as a sport and the team (the Indian team) that they once loved. The controversies surrounding the IPL and the spot-fixing scandal involving Pakistani players in England had only added fuel to the fire.

The number and manner of advertisements in cricket were mentioned as another common irritant that made them feel 'put off' by televised cricket. The incessant banner ads that makeup almost half the screen by reducing the game window considerably 'makes me want to change the channel' said one respondent. He compared it to coverage of the English Premier League, in which there were not too many intrusive ads till half time, he pointed out. A few respondents agreed that they had nothing against the Twenty20 game, and in fact lauded cricket administrators for coming up with a cricket format to rival football, and that one could go to with friends after work and enjoy a riveting game with players of an international standing. But watching cricket on television, they averred, was 'irritating'. The over breaks, the repeated advertisements, the length of the one-day game, and the suspicion of corruption in every match: all contributed to their irritation, they agreed.

But when the group did discuss the game of cricket, it was with more than a superficial understanding. They commented on the abilities of certain batsmen to combat spin, made comments on field placements for specific batsmen, the amount of swing specific bowlers could get on certain pitches, etc.; and often ended up comparing present players with those they remembered as heroes from their childhood.

Emergence of a Sporting-Entertainment Complex

The sporting-entertainment complex—so painstakingly put together by those in the allied industries of sports, marketing, broadcast, and business—is a peculiar beast. It is at once a sporting arena for modern-day gladiators, an evening out for young people after a long day's work, a treasure trove of 'eyeballs' for advertisers and celebrities, and a semi-audible drone of evening television around dinner time. The sporting-entertainment complex has managed to transform the once sedately paced game of cricket into a platform for adrenaline-pumping action sequences like the IPL, in which cricket is but one of several treats on offer to the spectator. The IPL has been structured, deliberately and carefully, as a platform; not just for advertisers seeking more eyeballs, but also for businesses that need more brand recognition, business people who need to pad their public image, film stars who seek publicity, and for the Board to put on a cricket show in which India could never lose no matter which team won.

The IPL's platform has been constructed on the foundation of television and Information and Communication Technologies (ICTs) and assembled by bringing together several diverse building blocks. It is through advertisements, fantasy league games, live streaming on mobile phones, publicity on social networking sites such as Facebook and Twitter, and fan engagement through a variety of other measures such as merchandising, etc. that the IPL garners popularity. Cricket in the subcontinent is an immensely profitable venture precisely because of its immeasurable utility as a platform through which to channel all the aforementioned ways of marketing and brand building. No longer just a game, the IPL has become the kind of platform that can provide more 'eyeballs' than any other marketing gimmick.

The centre of attention of all these 'eyeball' seekers is the spectator who watches the spectacle being produced upon this platform. Created on a substrate of ICTs such as the internet and broadcast media, the platform brings to the spectator—the fan, the consumer, the flâneur alike— a version of the sport of cricket that is profitable to those organizing it. Giulianotti's categories of fans and flâneurs place in perspective those for whom the platform is assembled. The IPL is specially designed to catch the attention of the roving entertainment seeker, whether idly channel surfing on a television in the living room or the stadium-going ticket buyer who gets a chance to click a 'selfie' with his or her favourite star in the background.

While it has been argued that the vast amount of technology that creates and brings us the sport of cricket has enhanced the viewing experience, what with Hawk-eye and spider-cams and Umpire-vision cameras, the main draw of the spectacle remains the carnivalesque atmosphere of the event driven by celebrity and non-stop action. The *tamasha* that so many observers of the game have commented on is the main draw of the IPL. Set up particularly to appeal to the non-traditional cricket fan, and to attract more and newer members to the cricket carnival, the IPL has been richly peppered with controversy (such as the much-publicized slapping incident involving S. Sreesanth and Harbhajan Singh[29]), gossip (Virat Kohli's encounters with his partner, movie star Anushka Sharma in 2015[30]), and scandal (Shah Rukh Khan's altercation with a security guard at Wankhede stadium, and his consequent banning in 2012[31]).

The target audience for the IPL is the urban middle-class consumer with a fairly large disposable income and immense purchasing power. This urbane cosmopolitan fan belonging to the new middle class of India enjoys the idea of the best international players playing for teams such as Kolkata and Chennai; and relishes the prospect of an evening out with friends at an event with food, drinks, music, cheering, and celebrities.

5

Technology, Speed, and Consumerism

In an interview with Gideon Haigh,[1] he told me the story of how when Cricket Australia (CA) was setting up the Big Bash League (BBL, the Australian professional franchise Twenty20 cricket league set up 2011), he had been quite critical of the idea of the BBL; and was invited to visit them to 'have a chat' about it. CA had apparently conducted extensive market research that showed that the BBL was a good idea. While the research showed that T20s were indeed a spectator favourite, encouraging the Board to set up the BBL, that wasn't the whole story. One of the questions in the survey, Haigh told me, had been something on the lines of what sort of cricket people wanted to watch more of, and 'the number one form that they wanted to see more of', Haigh said, 'was T20 internationals'. This is an opinion that is similar to what I have found in my conversations with many Indian spectators as well. In CA's survey, domestic T20s apparently ranked much lower than international T20s in terms of spectator interest. Why then, one might ask, are there so many domestic T20 leagues and so few T20 internationals?

Haigh thinks it's because cricket boards prefer to keep T20 as a domestic game. The popularity of the T20 game and the proposition of an alternative revenue stream for cricket boards makes domestic leagues an attractive option. An important other thing it can do is, in Haigh's words, 'you can mitigate your dependence on Indian tours. Because basically, Indian tours or a visit from the Indian team keeps a lot of these boards going. And your prosperity is dependent on how often you can play India'. The IPL model of a 'super-national' domestic T20 tournament that can bring in advertising and other revenue can help cricket boards make good money, when they are not playing an India series.

'Super-national' is a good way to describe the IPL. Essentially a domestic tournament, with high stakes in terms of its marketing and advertising reach, the international players who flock to it, and even the

Speeding up Sport. Vidya Subramanian, Oxford University Press. © Oxford University Press 2022.
DOI: 10.1093/oso/9780192865120.003.0006

visibility opportunities for domestic players hoping to 'make it' to the big leagues; the IPL is a massive money-making opportunity for the BCCI. It has inspired several other such domestic T20 leagues, but it remains the biggest one of them all. Azhar Habib of Wild Track Productions pegged the IPL as one of the biggest productions in all of world cricket. 'Probably the World Cup Final might be bigger in terms of scale of production, but in general IPL is probably one of the biggest', he told me.

A team of more than 500 people works on production and broadcast in the IPL. With 34 cameras, 'kilometres and kilometres of cabling' at every stadium, and other separate teams for graphics and other technologies that make up the television broadcast, the IPL is a massive production, like nothing else in cricket. The televised experience of the IPL is intended to be the main mode of engagement with it, but this does not mean that the stadium crowd is unimportant. The in-stadium crowd is an important part of the spectacle. Even though the stadium goers aren't the main spectators of the sport any longer, the stadium crowds, as Haigh put it, 'are still quite important in adding to the sense of spontaneity and occasion'. He went on to say that 'the spectators in the ground, in a way, sell the spectacle almost as much as the players … It's impossible to imagine the IPL without the great, demonstrative, heaving crowd responding to the cues that the organisers provide'. And there are many cues. There is music, there are announcements, the big screen showing different parts of the stadium and the signature IPL tune played at intervals to rousing cheers from the crowd.

Being at the Stadium

My experience of watching an IPL match in a stadium was exactly what I was told it would be like—a party. I had had the immense good fortune of meeting a senior bureaucrat who happened to have, and very generously gave away to me, two 'passes' to watch a match at the Ferozshah Kotla in Delhi in 2014; and that meant that the seats my friend and I found ourselves in were—to us—something amazing.

We were seated in a plexiglass enclosure right behind the visitors' dugout as the Delhi Daredevils took on the Sunrisers Hyderabad. The dressing room that cricket fans are familiar with, has been, in the IPL, augmented by the 'dugout', which is an opportunity for spectators, both in the stadium and on television, to see more of the stars that the teams boast of on the field. Right behind the section where our assigned seats were, were picnic tables, a sumptuous buffet, and as we discovered only after the tenth over, even free alcohol. It eventually turned out to be a rain-affected match that was decided by the Duckworth-Lewis system, but the cricket was only peripherally of interest in what was quite a fun evening.

The rain was somewhat upsetting to those who were interested in the match—many people stood around discussing the points table, Delhi's place in it, and the effect that this match would have on it—but the alcohol and food kept most spirits up in the section of the stadium I was in. The home team weren't the favourites, and many thought the Chennai Super Kings or the Mumbai Indians had a better chance of winning overall. I asked several people—including children and teenagers—who their favourite team in the IPL was, and not a single one said Delhi Daredevils. It all wound down quickly enough, and if weren't for the badly managed traffic right outside the stadium, the mud and slush in the aftermath of the downpour, and the post-rain traffic jams, the evening would have been a lot shorter.

The cricket itself seemed to have been a very small part of the evening, even allowing for the shortening of the match because of rain and Messrs Duckworth and Lewis. It hadn't felt like a cricket match at all. The Daredevils had scored 143 in their 20 overs, and the second innings had been curtailed first to 117 in 15 overs, and then 97 off 12 overs, and after yet another delay, the entire second innings was reduced to just five overs. The Sunrisers needed to make 43 runs in 5 overs, and they did it with 4 balls to spare. As we poured out of the stadium into the muddy sludge outside, no one seemed particularly cut up about the home side's loss; the second innings hadn't really felt like an 'innings' at all; but we had all seen Dale Steyn bowl and Kevin Pietersen bat, there had been food and drink, there were photos of the experience in our phones and our social media timelines, and it looked like everyone had had some fun . . . and many of us had not even had to pay for any of it!

Collapsing Space

Writing on the subject of politics and war, French cultural theorist Paul Virilio in *Speed and Politics* describes speed as resulting in a compression of space. Much of Virilio's work tries to analyse the consequences of the acceleration of technology on the society in which it is conceived. In a world of perpetual motion, he argues, speed has become important by itself and not just a facilitator for communication or transport. Our cities, he maintains, are built to encourage greater speeds, without necessarily needing to; movement and speed of communication have become ends in themselves, and a 'dictatorship of movement' has replaced the 'freedom of movement'.[2] Virilio suggests that in the relentless pursuit of speed (*dromos*, from the Greek), the destination becomes insignificant, and in many ways irrelevant. 'We are losing our sense of space', he declares. Speed as the rationale for itself will lead, he seems to imply, to a self-inflicted implosion as the only possible end. In order to keep up with this continuous quest for greater speed, Virilio argues, the dromomaniac experiences a disconnect with space. In writing of the new records set by Olympians, he observes:

> ... those Olympic champions whose records first progressed by hours, then by minutes, then by seconds, then by fractions of seconds. The better they performed (the more rapid they became), the more pitiful were the advances they obtained, until they could only be noticed electronically. One day, the champion will disappear in the limits of his own record ... For the dromomaniac, the engine is also a prosthesis for survival.

This appears to imply that the only way to bridge this disconnect between space and time—that has been brought about by speed—is through the mediation of technology. Feeding the frenzy of a new fidgety 'instant-everything' generation, technology becomes essential to T20 cricket: matches that become almost impossible to imagine and engage with without spider cameras, Hawk-Eye, and information technology. Test cricket, on the other hand, was not intentionally designed to be technologically mediated. It offered the tactile presence of the stadium and the visceral guts and sweat drama of an unmediated experience.

Slowness almost characterized play; liberally peppered as it was with drinks breaks, lunch, tea, and gaps between overs. In this commercialized televised format of cricket, some of the stadium experience can be said to have been lost.

I spoke to a self-confessed 'not very enthusiastic' cricket fan, who had been to the cricket stadium for the first time for a World Cup match in New Delhi in 2011. She sheepishly confessed to me that she had been surprised that at the end of every over, the wicketkeeper would have to run down to the other side of the pitch; and the field would have to be re-set with players on the leg side taking offside positions and vice versa. While she had always known ('obviously', she said) that there were two ends to a pitch and each over was bowled from alternate ends, the advertisement breaks never showed the changing of ends. And the first time that it happened in the stadium, she had been a bit confused about what was happening. In the mind of this spectator, the 'space' of the cricket match was never an actual stadium. It was a two-dimensional screen. It looked and felt exactly like everything else on television.

Virilio draws our attention to the 19th and 20th centuries and the transport and technological revolutions that came about in these 200 odd years. These transport and technological advances, he suggests, helped create a dromological state in which increased speed has led to the near elimination of distances between places.[3] The cost of this speed, he contends, is the 'negation of space itself'. This theory is taken a step further when he theorizes that dissent and resistance against the powers that be are now rendered futile since the 'occupation' of any given territory has now been supplanted by a more complete satellite surveillance of the whole planet. According to Patrick M. Bray,

> When speed becomes the driving force of progress, time compresses to the instantaneous, forcing all choices to be made in real time, without the benefit of extended reflection. Chains of command and control must be automated in order to avoid the mistakes of split-second decisions; machines are no longer products of human reason, but rather human bodies are subject to the reason of machines.

Thus shaping the idea of the politics of speed, Virilio also extends the theory to the highly mediatized world we inhabit today. Virilio warns of the dangers of the 'illusion of movement that occurs with the rapid succession of images', and invokes a condition of 'picnolepsy', in which 'a subject undergoes momentary lapses of memory and must continually reconstruct a narrative based on the fragmentary evidence that remains'. Virilio is extremely critical of cinema (or television), in which a series of still images move at the speed of several frames per second, giving the impression of continuous movement. 'For Virilio', writes Bray, 'the film or television spectator, and therefore all of us, becomes a "picnolept", giving up a little bit of consciousness multiple times a second. The illusion of real time presence created by cinema or television masks a real, and nearly constant, disappearance of perception'.

Picnolepsy, in Virilio's theory, is as much about the loss of time as it is about the disappearance or impermanence of the image. In his words, 'Our vision is that of a montage, a montage of temporalities which are the product not only of the powers that be, but of the technologies that organize time'.[4] Writing about video games and Virilio's idea of speed, Rebecca Carlson and Jonathan Corliss point to Virilio's analysis of 'audio-visual vehicles' such as the constant stream of 'live' broadcasts of images and information on television screens, instantaneous global communication via the internet, and the continuous transmission of data around the globe.[5] The consumer of the 'audio-visual spectacles' is compared to the passive commuter on a train or bus who is a spectator to the landscapes that hurtle by just beyond the transparent window, and is according to Virilio, 'doomed to inertia'. Carlson and Corliss quote Virilio from his 1997 work *Open Sky* as having said:

> Even the latest supersonic fighter aircraft are designed around the cockpit—or, in other words, around the instrument panel and ejector seat of the 'elite pilot' who has become the perfect example of the disabled person, his very survival depending upon the motor and audio-visual feats of his equipment.

This technological dependence, Virilio appears to suggest, is what creates a disconnect with the lived reality of life, putting the consumer/spectator into a sort of controlled stupor. In the words of Carlson and Corliss, 'The uncontrollable speed of motion, of transatlantic flights, of data along fibre optic cables, the dizzying rush from elevators rising hundreds of floors

into the sky, all this erases real space; our ability to sense this space, to an-
chor ourselves in it properly, to live in it'.

To extrapolate the theory to cricket, it can be speculated that as the
centre of the match is transposed from the game itself, it has become, as
Virilio outlines, a dromologically progressing state that is increasingly
disconnected from the space it once was part of. In so doing, the very
understanding of the game has had to be geographically reworked, with
the players being un-tethered from region and nation. Teams and players
of the IPL (and indeed in the several similar leagues that have sprung up
around the world) have been *bought* and their allegiance lies now foremost to their team owners. Players from several states and countries are
expected to play together for a very small part of the year in a team that
has little or nothing to do with where they *belong*. The fans, consequently,
pick their teams arbitrarily—based on favourite players, the celebrity
status of the team owners, or as brands that are expected to endure.

Cricket in a 'Liquid Modern' Age

Cricket analysts, including Ashis Nandy, C.L.R. James, and Ayaz Memon,
have often described cricket as being an accurate reflection of the society
in which it was played. In keeping with this view, they see the changes
in the game in the 1950s as mirroring the condition of society in these
years. In talking of the Golden Age, between 1890 and 1914, C.L.R. James
writes,

> The solid Victorian age was breaking up, the contemporary pattern had
> not taken shape, and in the interim ... we have these dynamic explo-
> sions of individual and creative personalities expressing themselves to
> the utmost limit in a manner impossible today.[6]

Memon too stresses this point as he compares post-War England's quest
for a new identity, the increase in importance of professionalism, and
a 'security-first' approach of the English people, to the same standards
being followed by players in English cricket as well.[7] The same analysis
has been used to explain the exponential rise of interest in cricket in
India. Nalin Mehta has written of the rise of cricket in India being linked

to the politics of identity, broader trends in globalization, and the birth of the satellite television industry.[8] With the success of the IPL and the increasing role of technology, the transformation of the game of cricket could also well reflect the transformations within the society itself.

Zygmunt Bauman, the Polish sociologist, has spoken of the modern-day citizen as living in a 'liquid modern' world, simultaneously as both a consumer and a commodity, where 'human bonds tend to lead through and be mediated by the market for consumer goods'.[9] It is possible to view these tenuous mediations as ones that could have arisen and been enabled by technological influxes. It can, thereby, just as well be argued that the game of cricket too is a commodity to be consumed, along with the latest cell phone technologies, lifestyle choices, holiday destinations, the personality cult, and everything else that is advertised. Bauman argues that nothing in the liquid modern world (a world in which individuals constantly 'stagger under the weight of an accumulation of consumer culture'[10]) is uncommodifiable. Commodified sport then becomes just one of the several things that can be consumed. Bauman describes 'consumption' as using and then discarding the *item* until a *better* version comes along. He speaks of the inherent injection of speed into the proceedings in this 'nowist' way of life and its constant 'necessity to discard and replace'.[11]

After Kerry Packer took mainstream cricket into television, the result of the match has become more important than the playing out of it. And as the evolution of cricket has reached the IPL, television has been critical to redesigning the format, not only to conquer prime viewership as a sport but also as entertainment trying to out-eyeball reality shows and soap operas. In the words of Michael Miller, 'Spectacle and entertainment on one hand, and the world of consumption, on the other, were now truly indistinguishable'.[12] The individualization of the sport, then, becomes a crucial frontier in the first stages of commodification. To this end, the techniques, technologies, and calculations used to meet the logic of commodification have perhaps been most emphatically and profoundly crucial in shaping the IPL format.

The IPL, sold as an 'improved' version of cricket, was centrally aimed at convincing advertisers and corporate sponsors that it provided an unprecedented opportunity to increase 'eyeballs' for their products. And in order to be appealing to this new society of consumers, cricket was transformed into another of the several commodities that could be *consumed*. The spectator of the sport thus became a *consumer* of the game, and watching a cricket match became equivalent to buying into the concepts and philosophies of the new universe of cricket—that of products, brands, glamour, etc. Even the commentary box has been roped into the marketing of the game: from describing the game to hyping product and brand value. Writing on the commentators' new role, Osman Samiuddin shows how commentary became PR, as commentators described each six as a 'DLF Maximum' and every important turning point as a 'Citi Moment of Success'.[13] Commentary, thus, was now an advertisement itself—shepherding consumption and orienting brand focus.

A case in point is the 2014 FIFA World Cup held in Brazil, where FIFA even managed to influence the Brazilian Parliament to pass a law to favour their sponsors.[14] To tackle violence and hooliganism among rival football fans in Brazil, the sale of beer during football matches had been illegal since 2003. But since Budweiser was one of the important sponsors of the event, FIFA 'made it clear that the right to sell beer must be enshrined in legislation on the World Cup in the Brazilian Congress'. Jerome Valcke, General Secretary of FIFA, even went so far as to say that, 'Alcoholic drinks are part of the FIFA World Cup, so we're going to have them. Excuse me if I sound a bit arrogant but that's something we won't negotiate … The fact that we have the right to sell beer has to be a part of the law'. Toeing the line, the Brazilian Parliament then signed into law a bill that, in principle, overturned the ban on the sale of beer at football matches.

Even as televised sport provides a great channel for marketing, it provides an enormous opportunity for individual celebrity. Close-ups of the individual and the ability to transform every moment into a dramatic slow-motion replay make television a potent tool for a celebrity to cash in on their own fame, and indeed to create it. Take, for instance a Jonty Rhodes catch in mid-air. It is magnificent any way one cuts it, but in slow motion, the impossible angles of his body, his unmatched agility, and the drawn-out drama of the catch make it so much more spectacular.

This focus on individual celebrity has helped construct the modern-day sportsperson as a brand in himself (or indeed herself. Sportspersons like Serena Williams in Tennis and Saina Nehwal in badminton are recognized, saleable faces in the worlds of endorsements and marketing). The promotion, management, and positioning of the brand of a sportsperson have spawned an entire industry of sports management, thus proving the importance of sport to business and of business to sport.

Theorizing Consumption

Tracing the origins of consumption, Bauman reiterates that 'all people at all times did and do' consume. Like all living creatures, humans have always consumed to stay alive, he avers. However, he argues, 'being alive in the human way set demands which topped the necessities of "merely *biological*" existence with more elaborate *social* standards of decency, propriety, 'good life'". Survival, both biological and social, was the primary purpose of consumption in a pre-consumer society. It would have been irresponsible of a member of a pre-consumer society to consume less than he was expected to, and frowned upon if he flaunted his wealth by conspicuously consuming more. In a consumer society, however, consumption becomes its own purpose, becoming self-propelling, having given up the *need* aspect of consuming. It is no longer an activity *needed* for survival, he argues; instead, it becomes driven by something more transient—desire. Bauman argues:[15]

> The *spiritus movens* of consumer activity is not a set of articulated, let alone fixed, needs, but *desire*—a much more volatile and ephemeral, evasive and capricious, and essentially non-referential phenomenon; a self-begotten and self-perpetuating motive that calls for no justification or apology either in terms of an objective or a cause. Despite its successive and always short-lived reifications, desire is 'narcissistic': it has itself for its paramount object, and for that reason is bound to stay insatiable ... The 'survival' at stake is not that of the consumer's body or social identity, but of the desire itself: that desire which makes the consumer—the *consuming desire* of consuming.

Commodification creates an insatiable desire for consumption. It appears as though it is this ephemeral, evasive, and narcissistic desire that the sporting-entertainment complex aims to stoke in the minds of the spectator-consumer. Bauman further argues that promoters of commodities work hard—investing 'time, effort, and considerable financial outlay'—in order to 'arouse desire, bring it to the required temperature, and channel it in the right direction' in their audience. Such consumers must, he avers, be continuously 'produced'.

However, having defined the impetus of modern consumerism as 'desire', Bauman then goes a step further articulating the inadequacy of desire to 'muster enough power to keep the wheels of consumer society in motion'. While 'desire' was indeed more 'fluid' than the 19th century 'need', it has 'outlived its usefulness'. He writes:

> Desire has outlived its usefulness: having brought consumer addiction to its present state, it can no more keep pace. A more powerful and above all more versatile stimulant is needed to keep the acceleration of consumer demand on a level with the rising volume of consumer offer. 'Wish' is the much-needed replacement: it completes the liberation of the pleasure principle, purging the last residues of reality-principle impediments.

It is this consumer-driven behaviour that is reflected in the sports field as well. In the year before Sachin Tendulkar hung up his boots (after finally having completed a 100 centuries in international cricket), speculation abounded regarding his putting off his retirement, even as his performances on the field left much to be desired. From December 2011 to November 2013, in the 25 innings preceding his final series, Tendulkar scored four fifties, no centuries, and averaged less than 30 (more than 20 runs off his career average).[16] It went so far as to suggest that it was his sponsorship engagements that kept him from retiring from the game.[17] Notwithstanding the fact that the hundred hundreds landmark was used as a great advertising opportunity, alongside being a fitting crown to conclude a stellar career, brands he endorsed began considering a 'fee correction' given his extended poor form. A senior official at Toshiba said, 'Sachin's retirement should be a major concern for all brands. It's a major concern for us as well'. Sport and talent management experts even said that Tendulkar stood to lose a lot of endorsement money if he retired.

His final match, which made him the first cricketer in the history of cricket to have played 200 test matches,[18] was played at his home ground at the Wankhede in Mumbai. This match (and the series) was originally scheduled to be played outside the country—the scheduling of this India-West Indies series was hastily put together after postponing a tour to South Africa, in disregard of the ICC Future Tours Programme.[19] The series has even been called 'Sachin Tendulkar's farewell party'.[20] Tendulkar's 200th and final test match was eventually played in Mumbai in front of a packed stadium, filled with adoring fans, and—needless to say—a sizeable marketing opportunity and a major money-making event for the Indian cricket board.

As Dilip D'Souza points out in his book[21] *Final Test: Exit Sachin Tendulkar*, Tendulkar is possibly the only cricketer who had the opportunity to say goodbye to the game in the manner in which he did. The book details how the stadium was filled with adoring fans who came only to watch their hero play his final game. The match itself became secondary to the player, and spectators spent much time deliberating what needed to happen (including the collapse of the Indian team's remaining batsmen) to bring Tendulkar back to the crease. The West Indian team, he writes, had been reduced to 'no more than bridesmaids at the show'; but he points out they didn't mind very much, because playing in India, at this historic moment, in this very well-publicized event meant revenues that the West Indies cricket board could really use. The points of revenue generation were everywhere, as D'Souza points out: even in the banners that had been hung around the stadium's rafters proclaiming Tendulkar's centuries—they were sponsored by *Fair and Lovely Max Fairness*, a skin whitening product.

Cricket in Bauman's liquid modern world, it would appear, is more than a sport played to test the skills of one team over another, and not merely for the entertainment of its many fans. It is at once a sporting-entertainment complex with earning potential for advertisers, business people, and cricketers themselves; a sport that millions of fans enjoy; and a suitable buttressing aid for several allied industries such as player management, brand management (of players and businesses), technology companies, and even hospitality.

Teams in the IPL are also extremely active on social media and networking sites, with active Twitter handles, hashtag promotions, and fan interactions. After the 2014 edition of the IPL, the company Unmetric Technologies studied the 'the social performances' of all eight teams that were part of the IPL, and also measured the activities of the twelve major brands (Aircel, Amazon India, SpiceJet, Idea Cellular, Kingfisher, McDowells, Nokia India, Pepsi India, Quikr, Vodafone India, and YES Bank) that sponsored a team or the IPL itself to understand which team utilized social media most effectively or in their own words, 'who engaged the best by leveraging the tournament'.[22] An example of the metrics that are calculated is the awarding of the 'social trophy' to Kolkata Knight Riders. The Press Release reads, 'The team had the highest Facebook engagement, replied to the most tweets on Twitter and also uploaded the most new videos to their *YouTube* channel. With such a rounded social presence, their social media win cannot go unnoticed'. The brands have been evaluated too:

> *YES Bank* was the most talked about brand on Twitter. It was @-mentioned over 17,000 times in the 45 day period of the IPL. When it came to customer service on Twitter, Vodafone made over 6,000 replies (which is the most made by any IPL sponsor) while Kingfisher had the fastest fingers and replied to tweets in an average of three hours.

Thus, it would not be a big leap to conjecture that the networked media sport landscape is now populated by much more than the television screen. Social media and other information and communication technologies have spurred a new understanding of not just how to engage with the sport but also of how to measure the impact of the sport on businesses and their advertising campaigns through this new form of the sport.

Restructuring the Game

Critiques of the IPL tend to describe it as being a form of 'cricket-lite' or 'instant cricket' and a game specially designed for, as Ivo Tennant calls them, 'the modern, fidgety, fast-evolving society in which concentration levels are miniscule'.[23] IPL's 'instant' version of cricket, in such a scheme, appears to be a product of liquid modernity made for a society of distracted, fast-moving consumers. Speed then, not surprisingly, emerges as being almost as central to the game as the player on the field.

While technology has swept through most sports, the game of cricket has perhaps been most emphatically and profoundly re-shaped and re-structured by it. From being a game that was played over five days, to now rivalling a movie format in terms of time, the change in cricket has been, in a sense, overwhelming.

The changes in the game that have been spurred by technology—be it the television and related inventions, sports medicine, training equipment, or even software for analysis and broadcast such as the internet and social networking—have taken cricket from being a game to becoming a platform for several new constituencies, consequently creating a whole other beast. After Kerry Packer brought television into mainstream cricket, the influx of technology has shaped the way cricket has been engaged with. The latest innovation in cricket has been the emergence of Twenty20 cricket. T20 cricket and the IPL were aimed at giving prime-time TV watchers something similar enough to what was on already—reality TV shows with celebrities from business, cinema, and cricket, but this time with some speeded-up sporting action thrown in. Technologies such as spider cameras and mongoose bats gave an added injection of pace to the normal cricket action that TV viewers were used to.

In speaking of cricket being shaped by the medium (television), Gideon Haigh makes the point that the relationship between broadcast media and cricket has changed drastically. With the onus of fair play having shifted to the television camera, the moral centre of cricket too has shifted to technology. 'Before World Series Cricket the action dictated the coverage', he points out. 'The cameras were static and distant; replays were scarce, and seldom shown more than once. WSC introduced the idea of using the characters, the stories, their statistics and replay technology, to create a master narrative.'[24] He laments the loss of the specialist commentator, who was not necessarily an ex-player,

> There was no place for them (broadcasters without playing backgrounds) amid the hyperbole and histrionics of this new gladiatorial forum. The commentator in commercial media is selling the product. The commentator acts like a celebrity endorsement. When Sunil Gavaskar says a cover-drive is magnificent, it is like Sachin (Tendulkar) saying that Pepsi is refreshing'.

Reality TV 2.0?

A form of cricket that has been transformed into an industry, on which ride several other interests and stakeholders, is at its heart a little more than a game and a little less than a sport. Software engineers who can design better analytical software, film stars who seek publicity, players looking for quick money, businesses looking for a better advertising platform, and television channels trying to improve their ratings—can all find homes within the game of cricket today. As has been previously pointed out, the game of cricket itself is no longer the centre of the event of the match. There are so many other interests riding on each match that the sport itself seems to be growing in many directions at once—as a lucrative business, as an effective advertising medium, as a vehicle for individual celebrity, etc. In such a multi-focal universe, cricket is just one of the things in the mix.

In comparison to being the sport that Ashis Nandy described as a 'ritualised garden party',[25] cricket is today, first and foremost, a platform. Mediated by technology and driven by what can be called a need for speed, cricket has proved itself to be an excellent vessel for the promotion, development, and sustenance of several other industries. But it might perhaps also be said that it has, in the process, lost some of the space that it once occupied in the minds and hearts of some of its oldest fans.

Milan Kundera, in his book *Slowness*, describes technology as having a 'cold impersonality'.[26] He ties technology with speed, and goes on to describe the idea of speed in terms of 'existential mathematics' and two 'equations'. The first of these 'equations' is that 'the degree of slowness is directly proportional to the intensity of memory' and its consequent inverse is the second 'equation': 'the degree of speed is directly proportional to the intensity of forgetting'. Arguably, a strong version of slowness was intricately woven into the fabric of cricket in the heyday of the test match. In other sports such as tennis or football, breathtaking action was often continuous; the time spent on the entire match would be (even today) the equivalent of an afternoon out, and the result most often described the game.

Cricket now falls into the same fold of high-powered action sports. While the technical aspects of playing remain intricate and exciting, it has also become, as one fan put it, 'easier to watch'.[27] He was speaking of how it has become 'easier' to follow the game because of the manner in which the IPL is played. If you hit out or are getting a lot of wickets, you're playing well; and the other team is not. Changes in fortune add to the excitement. 'And it doesn't take five long days', he said drawing out the vowels in the last three words to emphasize the time aspect of the IPL and the T20 game. 'When a test match or even a one-dayer is on', he told me, 'we only check the score every two hours. I don't feel like watching unless I hear that someone is playing a great innings right now'.

In creating a purely domestic sporting league based on city affiliations that no longer tug at the heartstrings of patriotism and nationalism, the IPL has created a version of the game in which the fan appears to pledge loyalty to a brand—be that of a cricketer, or a film star 'owner' of a team, or indeed a favourite consumer trademark.

To an urban middle-class audience that seemingly enjoys the scripted immediacy and drama of reality television, Lalit Modi created a television spectacle that could sell a new brand of entertainment—complete with controversy, tabloid sensationalism, and gossip. The IPL has been created and runs as an effective platform, not just for advertisers looking for innovative ways to sell products but also for brands looking for recognition, celebrities who need a fillip in publicity, and for the Board to put an exciting cricket-based show that India would never lose no matter which team won.

Conclusion

'What do they know of cricket who only cricket know' asked the famous Trinidadian cricket writer C.L.R. James in his definitive cricket memoir *Beyond a Boundary*.[1] First published in 1963, the book is from a time when cricket was still played in white flannels and camera crews in stadia had not yet entered the cricketing imagination. *Beyond a Boundary* reflects on both the society of that time—its politics, class, race, and aesthetics—and the game of cricket as it was then played. This premise perhaps is as true today as it was then. Cricket in all its myriad shades, be it the loud fluorescence of the jerseys in the IPL or the shift in the power centre of the game from England to the subcontinent, appears to have consistently reflected the colours of society.

In studying how the IPL has been assembled as a sporting platform, I have attempted to make two unambiguous claims: a) that the game of cricket is the most important ingredient in the making of the IPL as a sporting platform and b) Technologies such as ICTs have enabled the creation of a new type of commodity for consumption through the politics of speed. I have attempted to study the present landscape of sport and entertainment in India through the lens of STS (Science, Technology, and Society) in order to understand how ICTs have shaped the IPL.

From Process to Product

Cricket is really the only game of its kind. It's as much a sport of endurance as it is of guile, strategy, and power. In a time long before the IPL-ization of cricket, it took five days for a single match to finish, and commentators compared the sport to theatre and ballet as much as to others sports. The result of the match was not considered the most important part of the game. The draw was not just an acceptable outcome, but in many cases,

Speeding up Sport. Vidya Subramanian, Oxford University Press. © Oxford University Press 2022.
DOI: 10.1093/oso/9780192865120.003.0007

was considered more exciting than a straight win/loss game—as much for the spectators as the sport's practitioners.

While it was always a spectacle, with huge spectator interest, the narrative of the sport was built slowly, through various media. From radio commentary to newspaper writings and then accompanying photographs, the story of cricket was told through a plural narrative. And the memory of the match perhaps lasted longer because of the way that it was stitched together, slowly and over a period of time. Slowness was built into the game structure itself, with drinks breaks every hour, tea and lunch on every day of play, and so was the narrative of the game built—slowly. Technological advances in other spheres of life—Ayaz Memon points out that the motor car and the television were 'two (of the) most powerful counter-attractions to all established forms of entertainment'.[2]—caused cricket to begin reflecting those shades as well, and as cricket audiences in stadia depleted in England, administrators began to explore new formats for an old game.

The Tentacles of Technology

In an age when cricket was played solely in the test match, five-day format, it remained largely unmediated by technology. As I have argued in Chapter 2, with the advent of television and other forms of engagement with the game, not only have two new formats of the game arisen (one-day and Twenty20) but also a continuous influx of technological mediation has occurred; be it in the dressing room in terms of training and preparation or in the realm of umpiring such as the third umpire and the Decision Review System.

Writing on one of Tennis' all-time greats Roger Federer, David Foster Wallace speaks of the difference between experiencing the sport on television and watching it in a stadium. 'TV tennis is to live tennis pretty much as video porn is to the felt reality of human love', he writes.[3] But even the lived reality of tennis in a stadium is mediated by a screen. Every line call challenge that is referred to Hawk-Eye* is applauded by those

---

* In International tennis, every player receives three challenges in a set to question a line call; and receives one additional challenge should a tie-break ensue. These challenges are referred to Hawk-Eye, which then displays on the big screen within the stadium, the trajectory of the ball.

present in the stadium and an audible cheer follows the trajectory of the ball as Hawk-Eye displays the visual on the large screen. In cricket, Hawk-Eye and third-umpire decisions are awaited by the stadium audience only to be seen on the large screens. Stadium audiences in cricket (and in other sports such as football) dress flamboyantly or perform a routine or hold up interesting banners to attract the attention of the camera person who is scouring the crowd for just such a visual. Thus, as Paul Virilio points out,[4] the stadium audience has been appropriated into the spectacle that is televised for millions around the world. It is thus that several researchers of sport have pegged the televised broadcast of sport as a whole other event from the one witnessed in the stadium.[5]

Several critiques of the game consider the question of how technology has made its way into cricket. In comparison with something like the Goal Line Technology in football which has been extensively tested, most of the technological aids in umpiring and in-game decision making in cricket have simply been inherited from broadcast technology.[6] Originally introduced to make the televised game more interesting for TV viewers, technological add-ons like HotSpot and Hawk-Eye have moved from broadcast to umpiring with almost no field testing at all.

Technological aids such as videographing allow even something as hands-on as coaching to become technologically mediated. So much so that the player and his coach need not even be in the same country for coaching to take place. This is not to suggest that the physical presence of the coach has been entirely done away with, but in cases where a personal coach is unable to travel with the player, information and communication technologies (ICTs) allow for even remote coaching to become a reality.

The Spectacle Is Televised

The world we inhabit today is populated by screen interfaces of all shapes and sizes—from LED TVs to smartwatches, from mobile phones to laptops, and from tablets to large screens at public places. It would seem as though our entire lived experience has somehow been flattened to fit into the two physical dimensions of a rectangle and constrained to the options that these many 'screens' provide. Be it communicating with friends or buying groceries, most of our experiences are mediated by invisible networks and visible screens. The experience of sport seems to be no different. Even the stadium experience is incomplete without the big screen and the possibility of being caught on camera and being seen on it.

To look at it from another angle, there is no successful sporting event without television. Even the Olympics are only considered a success when the event is held in a time zone that is friendly to western television audiences.[7] Chapter 3 argues that this makes television and the internet very potent tools in the hands of marketing wizards, who use events with large public followings such as Grand Slam tennis or the FIFA World Cup as vehicles for promotion. While it seems like a great idea for businesses to fund high-quality sports events simply at the cost of telling viewers who has funded the event, the commercialization of the sports event has now gone beyond anything that anyone could have imagined.

The growing use of second screen (laptops, tablets, and computers) and third screen (mobile phones) devices has enabled sport to become what is now called 'networked media sport'.[8] Sport and television have now become inseparable. The medium of television, as Gary Whannel has pointed out, is immensely suited to a 'close-up centred' method of programming that allows individual sportspersons to become recognizable stars and celebrities, consequently enhancing their earning potential from endorsements and advertising.[9] The televised sport is not just a sport. It has become, among other things, 'a branch of the advertising and promotion industry'.

Changing Landscape of Audiences

The spectator is at the centre of the show that television puts on. The chief 'audience' of a sporting event is, however, absent from the site of the spectacle. The stadium audience for a sporting event is a small part of the larger spectatorship. The manner in which an event, sporting or otherwise, is broadcast 'live' to millions of people around the world, changes the notion of the 'crowd' that exists at the heart of a spectacle. The 'crowd' now is all of those people watching the show on television, on the internet, and in public spaces, all put together. They may be sitting with friends, family, or alone, but have become part of the spectating 'crowd'. This fragmented, non-unified, and yet seemingly all-powerful 'crowd' belongs to what Paul Virilio has called the 'city of the instant'. This 'city' is a virtual space in which almost everyone, everywhere in the world can be watching an event 'live' on screens. This is explored in Chapter 4.

The metrics to gauge how the IPL was used as an advertising platform and who used social media 'effectively' is essentially a study of who was better able to engage the spectator, the fan. Users of social media who tweet to teams, tag pictures, and use hashtags are at the heart of the sporting-entertainment complex. They generate content in terms of Facebook posts, tweets, sharing videos, commenting, and enable companies, advertisers, PR agencies, and statisticians to understand how deeply engaged with the brands and other entities the audience can be.

Richard Giulianotti has categorized the viewing public for a football event, a sport that is primarily played by local clubs, into four types: supporters, followers, fans, and flâneurs.[10] While it is difficult to directly transpose these categories onto the spectators or the stadium crowds for cricket, the notion of cricket fandom in the subcontinent opens itself to some comparison. As argued in Chapter 4, the categories of 'follower' and 'fan' collapsed into one single category prove adequate to describe most traditional cricket fans, particularly in India. This is because the fandom for cricket is largely unidirectional, topophilic, and the engagement with the sport and teams is mainly through the electronic media.

Giulianotti's category of flâneurs is easily transposable to fans of the IPL. He describes the flâneur as typically usually male, adult, bourgeois, 'an idler and a traveller', 'an urban stroller ... (who) would promenade through boulevards and markets'. This could easily describe several fans of the IPL. The description of flâneurs as 'window shoppers' also describes fans of the IPL, who appear to be 'motivated to seek sensation, excitement, and thus to switch their gaze across clubs, players, and nations'. The IPL then, as Giulianotti suggests, 'encourages the germination of a proxy form of narcissistic self-identity for the cool consumers'.

The IPL has always been presented as an entertainment package. With explosive, nail-biting matches supplementing a theatre of celebrities, gossip, cheerleaders, glamorous presenters, movie promotions within matches, and even on-field interviews with players while they are playing; the IPL marks a crucial moment in the understanding of sport, television, and audiences in present-day India.

The Politics of Speed

Paul Virilio suggests that the transport and technological revolutions of the 19th and 20th centuries have helped create a dromological state in which increased speed has led to the near elimination of distances between places.[11] This increase in speed, Virilio argues, is paid for by the ' negation of space itself'. This theory is taken a step further when he theorizes that dissent and resistance against the powers that be are now rendered futile since the 'occupation' of any given territory has now been supplanted by a more complete satellite surveillance of the whole planet. Virilio points to the ever-shrinking margins of the new records set at the Olympics. He observes that even as sportspersons strive to be better than the records, the tinier are the actual advances on previous records. The margins, he says, are so miniscule, that 'they could only be noticed electronically'.[12] Virilio's argument essentially appears to be that as speed continues to increase, it creates a disconnect with the space on which it is created.

As discussed in Chapter 5, Virilio is extremely critical of the medium of television. He warns of the dangers of the 'illusion of movement that occurs with the rapid succession of images', and invokes a condition of 'picnolepsy', in which 'a subject undergoes momentary lapses of memory and must continually reconstruct a narrative based on the fragmentary evidence that remains'. The tactility and the real-world feel of a possibly messy, unforgiving life are replaced, for Virilio by 'the uncontrollable speed of motion, of transatlantic flights, of data along fibre optic cables, the dizzying rush from elevators rising hundreds of floors into the sky'.[13]

To extrapolate the theory to cricket, it can be speculated that as the centre of the match is transposed from the game itself, it has become increasingly disconnected from the space it once was part of. In so doing, the very understanding of the game has had to be geographically reworked, with the players being un-tethered from region and nation. Teams and have been *bought* and their allegiance lies now foremost to their team owners. Players from several states and countries are expected to play together for a very small part of the year in a team that has little or nothing to do with where they *belong*. The fans, consequently, pick their teams arbitrarily—based on favourite players, the celebrity status of the team owners, or as brands, which are expected to endure.

Zygmunt Bauman, speaking of the 'liquid modern' world we live in, believes that we all now exist both as consumers and commodities, where 'human bonds tend to lead through and be mediated by the market for consumer goods'.[14] He maps out the evolution of consumption from a time when it was a citizen's responsibility to consume enough to keep society functioning and conspicuous consumption was considered to be in poor taste, to a time when people no longer consume to fulfil a *need* but in fact to fulfil something more elemental such as *desire*.[15]

To keep the consumption engine running and the profit margins of corporations high enough, desire has been morphed into something even more ephemeral and volatile, more capricious and evasive: *wish*.[16] We buy not because we need to or we desire it, but simply because we *wish* to. A 'wish' that once denoted something almost impossible, something that was slightly out of reach, has been transformed to become a push to buy more, consume more.

The picnolepsy of the spectator, technologies of information and communication, the politics of speed inherent in the construction of the IPL as a sporting platform, and the ubiquity of screens as a manner of engagement with the rest of the world have created a world of sport in which disparate elements have come together and created a new situation that in many ways, is still unfolding. Studying the contemporary without the benefit of hindsight, it is impossible to say where the platform that cricket is, is headed. But it can no longer be ignored that cricket in India and the many fragilities and instabilities that it exhibits may not be inherent to the sport itself; but in fact, stem from the same technologies, consumerist attitudes, and the politics of speed that shape our society as a whole.

The target audience for the IPL is an urban middle-class consumer with a short attention span, a fairly large disposable income, and considerable purchasing power. The IPL sells to this audience a lifestyle that is in tune with the ideas of global brands and exotic vacations. With the emergence of a League such as the IPL, this cosmopolitan Indian cricket fan appears to be embracing more fully his other identity of a consumer, switching easily between brands, commodities, and IPL teams as the fortunes of one overtake another on the sporting, and indeed, advertising field.

Notes

Introduction

1. Nalin Mehta, Jon Gemmel, and Dominic Malcolm. '"Bombay Sport Exchange": Cricket, Globalisation, and the Future', *Sport in Society*, 12, no. 4/5 (May–June 2009), pp. 694–707.
2. Ramachandra Guha. 'Smash-and-Grab Crony League', *The Hindu*, 26 May 2012. http://www.thehindu.com/opinion/lead/smashandgrab-crony-league/article 3453046.ece (accessed 12 November 2015).
3. Alam Srinivas and T.R. Vivek. *IPL an Inside Story: Cricket and Commerce*. New Delhi: Roli Books, 2009.
4. Boria Majumdar. 'IPL Will Encourage Youngsters to Slog', *Dreamcricket.com*. 23 February 2008. http://www.dreamcricket.com/dreamcricket/news.hspl?nid= 8608&ntid=3 (accessed 21 December 2015).
5. Harsha Bhogle. 'Decoding the IPL Auction', on *ESPNCricinfo*, 14 January 2011. http://www.espncricinfo.com/magazine/content/story/496593.html?wrapp (accessed 12 November 2015).
6. Amit Gupta. 'India and the IPL: Cricket's Globalised Empire', *The Round Table*, 98 9April 2009), p. 401.
7. Mike Marqusee. 'Cashing in on Cricket', *The Hindu*, 9 March 2008. http://www. thehindu.com/todays-paper/tp-features/tp-sundaymagazine/cashing-in-on-cricket/article1437094.ece (accessed 21 November 2015).
8. Donald A. MacKenzie and Judy Wajcman. *The Social Shaping of Technology*. Open University Press, 1999.
9. Wiebe E. Bijker and John Law. *Shaping Technology/Building Society: Studies in Sociotechnical Change*. MIT Press, 1994.
10. Arturo Escobar. 'Welcome to Cyberia: Notes on the Anthropology of Cyberculture', *Current Anthropology*, 35, no. 3 (June 1994), pp. 211–231.
11. Sheila Jasanoff (Ed.). 'Ordering Knowledge, Ordering Society', in *States of Knowledge: The Co-Production of Science and the Social Order*. Routledge, 2004.
12. Paul Virilio. *Speed and Politics*. Translated by Mark Polizzotti. New York: Semiotext (e), 1986, p. 94.
13. Ramachandra Guha. *A Corner of a Foreign Field: The Indian History of a British Sport*. Picador India, 2002.
14. Ramachandra Guha. 'Litany of Loss', *Rediff Sports*, 23 September1998. http:// www.rediff.com/sports/1998/oct/16b.htm (accessed 21 November 2015).

126 NOTES

15. Ramachandra Guha. 'Varieties of the Game', *The Telegraph*, 29 March 2008. http://ramachandraguha.in/archives/varieties-of-the-game.html (accessed 20 January 2020).

16. Ashis Nandy. 'The Tao of Cricket', in *A Very Popular Exile*. New Delhi: Oxford University Press, 2007.

17. Ibid.

18. Boria Majumdar, 'Soaps, Serials and the CPI (M), Cricket Beat Them All: Cricket and Television in Contemporary India', *Sport in Society*, 11, no. 5 (September 2008), pp. 570–582.

19. Majumdar. 'IPL Will Encourage Youngsters to Slog'.

20. Nalin Mehta. 'Batting for the Flag: Cricket, Television and Globalization in India', *Sport in Society*, 12, no. 4 (May–June 2009).

21. Sanjay Joshi. 'Virtually There: Cricket, Community, and Commerce on the Internet', *International Journal of the History of Sport*, 24, no. 9 (September 2007), pp. 1226–1241.

22. Amit Gupta. 'The Globalization of Cricket: The Rise of the Non-West', *International Journal of the History of Sport*, 21, no. 2 (March 2004), pp. 257–276.

23. Harry Collins and Robert Evans. 'You Cannot Be Serious! Public Understanding of Technology with Special Reference to "Hawk-Eye"', *Public Understanding of Science*, 17, no. 3 (July 2008), p. 11.

24. Günther Lüschen. 'Sociology of Sport: Development, Present State, and Prospects', *Annual Review of Sociology*, 6 (1980), pp. 315–347.

25. Laura Nader. 'Up the Anthropologist: Perspectives Gained from Studying Up', in Dell H. Hymes (Ed.), *Reinventing Anthropology*. New York: Pantheon Books, 1972, pp. 284–311.

26. Ibid.

27. Interview with Pravin Amre (former India player and former assistant coach of the Pune Warriors India IPL team) conducted in 2012. He told me that several players (such as Robin Uthappa) have hired him to be their personal batting coach. On the day the interview was conducted in Mumbai, Uthappa was playing in a match outside the country.

28. Gupta. 'The Globalization of Cricket: The Rise of the Non-West'.

29. Brett Hutchins and David Rowe. *Sport Beyond Television: The Internet, Digital Media and the Rise of Networked Media Sport*. New York: Routledge, 2012.

30. Steve Redhead. 'Those Absent from the Stadium Are Always Right: Accelerated Culture, Sport Media, and Theory at the Speed of Light', *Journal of Sport and Social Issues*, 31, no. 3 (August 2007), pp. 226–241.

31. Ibid. Quotation from S. Lotringer and P. Virilio. *Pure War* (2nd ed.). New York: Semiotext (e), 1997.

32. Virilio. *Speed and Politics*.

33. Patrick M. Bray. 'Aesthetics in the Shadow of No Towers: Reading Virilio in the Twenty-first Century', *Yale French Studies*, 114 (2008), pp. 4–17.

34. Tony Blackshaw. *Zygmunt Bauman*. New York: Routledge, 2007, pp. 29–31.
35. Zygmunt Bauman. *Consuming Life*. Cambridge, UK: Polity Press, 2007, pp. 35–38.

Chapter 1

1. Ramachandra Guha. 'In defence of the draw', in *Scroll.in*. Reprinted from *The Telegraph* 1996. 12 January 2021. https://www.scroll.in/field/983817/ramachan dra-guha-in-defence-of-the-draw (accessed 15 January 2021).
2. Ashis Nandy. 'The Tao of Cricket', in *A Very Popular Exile*. New Delhi: Oxford University Press, 2007, p. 41.
3. C.L.R. James. *Beyond a Boundary*. London: Yellow Jersey Press, 2005, pp. 258–259.
4. Raju Bharatan. 'The Final Test of Strength'. *The Illustrated Weekly of India*, 4 February 1973, pp. 10–17.
5. Interview with Gideon Haigh, New Delhi. November 2014.
6. Martin Williamson. 'The Dawn of Television Coverage', on ESPNCricinfo. 5 August 2005. http://www.espncricinfo.com/magazine/content/story/214641. html (accessed 23 April 2011).
7. Christian Ryan. 'Cricket on the Radio', on ESPNCricinfo. 6 March 2010. http:// www.espncricinfo.com/magazine/content/story/450877.html (accessed 23 April 2011).
8. R. Mohan. 'India Pulls Off Incredible 59-run Victory'. *The Hindu*, 12 February 1981, p. 14.
9. James. *Beyond a Boundary*, p. 113.
10. Nandy. *The Tao of Cricket*. p. 21.
11. Milan Kundera. *Slowness*. United Kingdom: Faber and Faber, 1996, p. 34.
12. Ibid., p. 4.
13. Ayaz Memon. *Wills Book of Excellence: One-Day Cricket*. Kolkata (Calcutta), West Bengal: Orient Longman, 1992.
14. James. *Beyond a Boundary*, pp. 284–286.
15. Memon. *Wills Book of Excellence: One-Day Cricket*, p. 18.
16. Gordon Ross. 'Cricket's Strongest Wind of Change', in *Wisden Cricketers' Almanack*, via ESPNCricinfo. 1974. http://www.espncricinfo.com/wisdenalman ack/content/story/152767.html (accessed 21 March 2011)
17. Martin Williamson. 'The Birth of the One-Day International', on ESPNCricinfo. 22 June 2010. http://www.espncricinfo.com/magazine/content/story/464234.html (accessed 23 April 2011).
18. Memon. *Wills Book of Excellence: One-Day Cricket*, p. 168.
19. Williamson. 'A Brief history: World Series Cricket'.
20. 'The Packer Affair: ACB Brushed Their Friends Aside to Meet Their Own Ends', in *Wisden Cricketers' Almanack*, on ESPNCricinfo. 1980. http://www.espncricinfo. com/wisdenalmanack/content/story/152175.html (accessed 19 February 2011).

21. Trevor Bailey. 'The Helmet: Sensible Adjunct or Well-marketed Gimmick?', in *Wisden Cricketers' Almanack*, on ESPNCricinfo. 1981. http://www.espncricinfo.com/wisdenalmanack/content/story/153032.html (accessed 20 March 2011).

22. Ramachandra Guha. 'Varieties of the Game', in *The Telegraph*, 29 March 2008. http://ramachandraguha.in/archives/varieties-of-the-game.html (accessed 21 January 2020)

23. James. *Beyond a Boundary*, pp. 258–259.

24. Nandy. *The Tao of Cricket*, pp. 38–41.

Chapter 2

1. Martin Williamson. 'A Word in Your Ear', on *ESPNCricinfo*, 7 March 2015. http://www.espncricinfo.com/magazine/content/story/844455.html (accessed 5 July 2016).

2. Gideon Haigh. 'Aye, Aye, Coach: The Rise and Rise of the Backroom Boys', in *Wisden Cricketers' Almanack 2006* on *ESPNCricinfo*. http://www.espncricinfo.com/wisdenalmanack/content/story/247080.html (accessed 21 March 2015).

3. Peter English. 'From the Fringes to the Engine Room', on *ESPNCricinfo*, 31 December 2009. http://www.espncricinfo.com/decadereview2009/content/story/441759.html (accessed 11 June 2015).

4. John Buchanan's Profile on *ESPNCricinfo*. http://www.espncricinfo.com/australia/content/player/4233.html (accessed 11 June 2015).

5. Interview with Gideon Haigh, New Delhi. November 2014.

6. Nagraj Gollapudi. 'Zach Hitchcock, Video Analyst' in 'The Backroom Boys', on *ESPNCricinfo*. http://www.espncricinfo.com/magazine/content/story/238883.html (accessed 16 June 2015).

7. Interview with S. Ramakrishnan, 2010–11.

8. Sports Mechanics India (P) Ltd. is a Chennai-based firm, to be found online at www.sportsmechanics.in (https://web.archive.org/web/20150509082136/http://sportsmechanics.in/) (accessed 11 June 2015).

9. Sports Mechanics. 'Services'. http://sportsmechanics.in/services.aspx (https://web.archive.org/web/20150510092517/http://sportsmechanics.in/services.aspx) (accessed June 2015).

10. Cricket Mentor. 'About Us'. http://www.cricketmentor.tv/Aboutus.aspx (https://web.archive.org/web/20150204224027/http://www.cricketmentor.tv/Aboutus.aspx) (accessed 11 June 2015).

11. Cricket Mentor. 'Clientele'. https://web.archive.org/web/20110818064420/http://www.sportsmechanics.in/Clientele.html (accessed 21 June 2011).

12. English. 'From the Fringes to the Engine Room'.

13. Derek Pringle. 'The Appliance Of Science: A View from the Dressing Room' in *Wisden Cricketers' Almanack 1998* on *ESPNCricinfo*. http://www.espncricinfo.com/wisdenalmanack/content/story/153293.html (accessed 21 March 2015).

14. Interview with Murali Kartik New Delhi, in March 2013.
15. Derek Pringle. 'The Appliance Of Science: A View from the Dressing Room' in *Wisden Cricketers' Almanack 1998 on ESPNCricinfo.* http://www.espncricinfo.com/wisdenalmanack/content/story/153293.html (accessed 21 March 2015).
16. Mukul Kesavan. 'Match Referee RIP'. *Wisden Asia Cricket,* January 2002. http://www.espncricinfo.com/wac/content/story/224747.html (accessed 19 June 2015).
17. John Woodcock. 'Notes by the Editor' in *Wisden Cricketers' Almanack 1983* on *ESPNCricinfo.* http://www.espncricinfo.com/wisdenalmanack/content/story/153040.html (accessed 23 April 2015).
18. Raju Bharatan. 'The Final Test of Strength'. *The Illustrated Weekly of India,* 4 February 1973, pp. 10–17.
19. Ashis Nandy. 'The Tao of Cricket', in *A Very Popular Exile.* New Delhi: Oxford University Press, 2007, p. 41.
20. Scyld Berry. 'Notes by the Editor', in *Wisden Cricketers' Almanack 2008* on *ESPNCricinfo.* http://www.espncricinfo.com/wisdenalmanack/content/story/344613.html (accessed 21 March 2015).
21. Nandy. 'The Tao of Cricket', pp. 38–41.
22. C.L.R. James. *Beyond a Boundary* (1963). London: Yellow Jersey Press, 2005, pp. 56–58.
23. Ranjit Fernando. 'Third Umpire: Some Thoughts'. *Sportstar,* June 23–29, 2001. Vol. 24(25). https://www.sportstar.thehindu.com/magazine/third-umpire-some-thoughts/article29634195.ece (accessed 25 April 2015).
24. Ivo Tennant. 'The Tentacles of TV', on *ESPNCricinfo,* 1 March 2001. http://www.espncricinfo.com/innovation/content/story/503609.html (accessed 21 March 2015).
25. Nick Hoult. 'Everything You Need to Know about How Cricket Technology Works'. *The Telegraph,* 7 August 2013. http://www.telegraph.co.uk/sport/10229593/Everything-you-need-to-know-about-how-cricket-technology-works.html (accessed 19 June 2015).
26. Ivo Tennant. 'Empowered or Undermined', on *ESPNCricinfo,* 22 March 2011. http://www.espncricinfo.com/innovation/content/story/507398.html (accessed 14 June 2015).
27. 'X-Ray Vision', on *ESPNCricinfo,* 4 August 2008. http://www.espncricinfo.com/ci/content/story/362371.html (accessed 21 April 2015).
28. Simon Hughes. 'An Eye to the Future', in *Wisden Cricketers' Almanack 2002* on *ESPNCricinfo.* http://www.espncricinfo.com/wisdenalmanack/content/story/154890.html (accessed 21 March 2015).
29. Harry Collins and Robert Evans. 'You Cannot Be Serious! Public Understanding of Technology with Special Reference to Hawk-Eye'. *Public Understanding of Science,* July 2008. Vol. 17(3).
30. Tennant. 'Empowered or Undermined'.
31. Nagraj Gollapudi. 'Government Says It Can't Provide IPL Security during Polls'. https://www.espncricinfo.com/story/government-says-it-can-t-provide-ipl-security-during-polls-721055 (accessed 15 October 2015)

32. *ESPNCricinfo* Live Scores. 'Pepsi Indian Premier League, 14th Match: Rajasthan Royals v Royal Challengers Bangalore at Abu Dhabi, Apr 26, 2014'. https://www.espn.com/cricket/series/8048/commentary/729305?innings=2&filter=full (accessed 27 January 2016).

33. Tennant. 'Empowered or Undermined'.

34. Shweta. *Commercialisation of Cricket in India: A Study in the Sociology of Sport*, M.Phil Dissertation 2006. Centre for the Study of Social Systems, Jawaharlal Nehru University.

35. Tennant. 'The Tentacles of TV'.

36. Owen Gibson. 'Cricket May Have Embraced Technology too Quickly, Says Hawk-Eye Founder'. *The Guardian*, 8 August 2013. http://www.theguardian.com/sport/2013/aug/08/cricket-embraced-technology-hawkeye-founder (accessed 15 June 2015).

37. Telegraph Sport. 'Ashes 2013: Kevin Pietersen Denies Australian Reports He May Have Used Silicone Tape to Deceive Hot Spot'. *The Telegraph*, 7 August 2013. http://www.telegraph.co.uk/sport/cricket/international/theashes/10226690/Ashes-2013-Kevin-Pietersen-denies-Australian-reports-he-may-have-used-silicone-tape-to-deceive-Hot-Spot.html (accessed 25 August 2015).

38. Mike Selvey. 'DRS Needs Urgent Overhaul So We Can Get on with Watching the Ashes'. *The Guardian*, 7 August 2013. http://www.theguardian.com/sport/blog/2013/aug/07/drs-urgent-overhaul-ashes (accessed 25 August 2015).

39. Internet World Stats 2020 Q3. http://www.internetworldstats.com/stats.htm. (accessed 5 January 2020).

40. IAMAI and Nielsen. 'Digital in India 2019 Round 2 Report'. https://reverieinc.com/wp-content/uploads/2020/09/IAMAI-Digital-in-India-2019-Round-2-Report.pdf

41. Boria Majumdar. 'Soaps, Serials and the CPI (M), Cricket Beat Them All: Cricket and Television in Contemporary India'. *Sport in Society*, September 2008. Vol. 11(5), pp. 570–582.

42. Sut Jhally, 'Cultural Studies and the Sports/Media Complex', in L. A. Wenner (Ed.), *Media, Sports, and Society*. California: Sage, 1989, pp. 70–93.

Chapter 3

1. http://www.youtube.com/embed/4tqBJvtvm7A?rel=0&start=12&end=88&autoplay=1

2. Aldous Huxley. *Brave New World* (1932). New York, NY: HarperCollins, 2006.

3. Amit Gupta. 'The Globalization of Cricket: The Rise of the Non-West', *International Journal of the History of Sport*, 21: 2 March 2004, pp. 257–276.

4. Vijay Lokapally. 'RIP Cricket', *The Hindu Business Line*, 11 April 2014. http://www.thehindubusinessline.com/features/blink/rip-cricket/article5900351.ece (accessed 13 September 2015)

5. Interview with G. Rajaraman, 2014

6. Garry Whannel. 'Television and the Transformation of Sport', *Annals of the American Academy of Political and Social Science, Vol. 625, The End of Television? Its Impact on the World (So Far)*, September 2009, pp 205–218.

7. Bharat Sharma. 'MS Dhoni Retires from Tests: Retirement from Tests Won't Affect His Brand, Believes Prasoon Joshi', *Cricketcountry.com*, 30 December 2014. http://www.cricketcountry.com/news/ms-dhoni-retires-from-tests-retirement-from-tests-wont-affect-his-brand-believes-prasoon-joshi-231024 (accessed 04 January 2016).

8. Michael Long. '50 Most Marketable 2013', *Sportspromedia.com*, 8 May 2013. http://www.sportspromedia.com/notes_and_insights/the_worlds_50_most_marketable_2013/ (accessed 20 January 2015).

9. David Cushnan. 'The World's Most Marketed Athletes', *Sportspromedia.com*, 19 May 2014. http://www.sportspromedia.com/notes_and_insights/the_worlds_most_marketed_athletes (accessed 20 January 2015).

10. Michael Long. '50 Most Marketable 2014', *Sportspromedia.com*, 12 May 2014. http://www.sportspromedia.com/most_marketable (accessed 20 January 2015).

11. Kevin Pietersen. *KP: The Autobiography*. Sphere Publications, 2014.

12. BBC Media Centre. 'Kevin Pietersen to Guest on Test Match Special Commentary Team', 4 February 2015. http://www.bbc.co.uk/mediacentre/latestnews/2015/cricket-world-cup (accessed 7 June 2015).

13. Paddy Power. 'Kevin Pietersen's Ashes Predictions', 6 July 2015 (accessed 19 June 2015) https://youtu.be/88lyifXTlw8.

14. Gideon Haigh. 'Controlling the Message', on *ESPNCricinfo*, 7 October 2013. http://www.espncricinfo.com/magazine/content/story/677319.html (accessed 15 October 2013).

15. Interview with Azhar Habib, August 2014

16. Osman Samiuddin. 'Sold Out', on *ESPNCricinfo*, 13 June 2008. http://www.espncricinfo.com/magazine/content/story/354158.html (accessed March 21, 2011).

17. Ayaz Memon. *Wills Book of Excellence: One-Day Cricket*. Kolkata (Calcutta), West Bengal: Orient Longman, 1992, pp. 62–66.

18. Martin Williamson. 'World Series Cricket' on *ESPNCricinfo*. http://www.espncricinfo.com/worldseries/content/story/72632.html (accessed March 21, 2011).

19. Gordon Ross. 'The Packer Case' in *Wisden Cricketers' Almanack* 1978 on *ESPNCricinfo*, http://www.espncricinfo.com/wisdenalmanack/content/story/152098.html (accessed 19 February 2011).

20. 'The Packer Affair: Long-drawn-out Saga Rolls Relentlessly on' in *Wisden Cricketers' Almanack* 1979 on *ESPNCricinfo*. http://www.espncricinfo.com/wisdenalmanack/content/story/152138.html (accessed 19 February 2011).

21. Memon. *Wills Book of Excellence: One-Day Cricket*, p. 66.

22. Tony Lewis in *The Sunday Telegraph* quoted in "The Packer Affair: ACB Brushed Their Friends Aside to Meet Their Own Ends" in *Wisden Cricketers' Almanack*

1980 on *ESPNCricinfo*. http://www.espncricinfo.com/wisdenalmanack/content/story/152175.html (accessed 19 February 2011).

23. Memon. *Wills Book of Excellence: One-Day Cricket*, p. 66.

24. 'The Packer Affair: ACB Brushed Their Friends Aside to Meet Their Own Ends' in *Wisden Cricketers' Almanack* 1980 on *ESPNCricinfo*. http://www.espncricinfo.com/wisdenalmanack/content/story/152175.html (accessed 19 February 2016).

25. Ivo Tennant. 'The Tentacles of TV', on *ESPNCricinfo*, 1 March 2001. http://www.espncricinfo.com/innovation/content/story/503609.html (accessed 21 March 2016).

26. Memon. *Wills Book of Excellence: One-Day Cricket*, p. 68.

27. Gideon Haigh. 'A Price for Everything' on *ESPNCricinfo*. http://www.espncricinfo.com/magazine/content/story/323297.html (accessed March 21 2011).

28. Vidya Subramanian. 'Cricket in the Fast Lane: Politics of Speed'. *Economic and Political Weekly*, 15 December 2012, pp. 21–24.

29. Alam Srinivas and T.R. Vivek. *IPL: An Inside Story: Cricket and Commerce*. New Delhi: Roli Books, 2009, p. 68.

30. Samiuddin. 'Sold Out'.

31. BCCI. 'Clothing and Equipment Regulations', *IPLT20*. 2014. https://web.archive.org/web/20140605005104/http://www.iplt20.com:80/about/2014/clothing-and-equipment-regulations/168/colours-and-design (accessed 20 August 2014).

32. Malcolm Conn. 'ICC, Players in for a Showdown Over Sponsorships', *The Hindu*, 5 June 2002. http://www.thehindu.com/2002/06/05/stories/2002060503101800.htm (accessed 24 December 2014).

33. Firstpost-Sports. 'There Was a Savage Attack on Me because I Have Dhoni: Srinivasan', *Firstpost*, 27 July 2013. http://www.firstpost.com/sports/there-was-a-savage-attack-on-me-because-i-have-dhoni-srinivasan-990567.html (accessed 21 August 2015).

34. PTI. 'Air India to Promote MSD and Others', *Hindustan Times*, 3 April 2011. https://web.archive.org/web/20130111140908/http://www.hindustantimes.com/news-feed/chunk-ht-ui-cricket-topstories/air-india-to-promote-msd-and-others/article1-680908.aspx (accessed 26 August 2014).

35. India Cements. https://web.archive.org/web/20140605074024/http://www.indiacements.co.in/careers.html (accessed 26 August 2014).

36. Guy Debord. *Society of the Spectacle*. Translated by Donald Nicholson-Smith. New York: Zone Books, 1994, p. 15. 'The spectacle manifests itself as an enormous positivity, out of reach and beyond dispute. All it says is: "Everything that appears is good; whatever is good will appear". The attitude that it demands in principle is the same passive acceptance that it has already secured by means of its seeming incontrovertibility, and indeed by its monopolization of the realm of appearances'.

37. Roger Silverstone. *Television and Everyday Life*. London: Routledge, 1994, p. 135.

38. Daniel Dayan and Elihu Katz. *Media Events: The Live Broadcasting of History*. Cambridge, Massachusetts: Harvard University Press, 1992.

39. Samiuddin. 'Sold Out'.
40. Debord. *The Society of the Spectacle*. p. 16.
41. Brett Hutchins and David Rowe. *Sport Beyond Television: The Internet, Digital Media and the Rise of Networked Media Sport*. New York: Routledge, 2012.
42. IPL. *Indian Premier League Tournament Handbook 2010*.
43. Hutchins and Rowe. *Sport Beyond Television: The Internet, Digital Media and the Rise of Networked Media Sport*, pp. 20–22.

Chapter 4

1. P.G. Wodehouse. *The Mating Season*. United Kingdom: Herbert Jenkins Ltd., 1949.
2. Gustave LeBon. *The Crowd: A Study of the Popular Mind* (1896). Kitchner: Batoche Books, 2001.
3. Steve Redhead. 'Those Absent from the Stadium Are Always Right: Accelerated Culture, Sport Media, and Theory at the Speed of Light', *Journal of Sport and Social Issues*, 31, no. 3 (August 2007), pp. 226–241.
4. Ibid. Quotation from S. Lotringer and P. Virilio, *Pure War* (2nd ed.). New York: Semiotext(e), 1997.
5. Vijay Santhanam and Shyam Balasubramanian. *If Cricket Is Religion, Sachin Is God*. Harper Collins India, 2009.
6. Satadru Sen. 'History Without a Past: Memory and Forgetting in Indian Cricket', in *Cricket and National Identity in the Postcolonial Age: Following On*, edited by Stephen Wagg. Routledge, 2005, pp. 94–109.
7. Steve Redhead. *Post-fandom and the Millennial Blues: The Transformation of Soccer Culture*. New York: Routledge, 1997.
8. Richard Giulianotti. 'Supporters, Followers, Fans, and Flâneurs: A Taxonomy of Spectator Identities in Football', *Journal of Sport & Social Issues*, 26, no. 1 (February 2002), pp. 25–46.
9. Cricinfo Staff. 'Lara Hopes Artistry Returns to Twenty20 Batting', on *ESPNCricinfo*, 8 April 2009. http://www.espncricinfo.com/westindies/content/story/398808.html (accessed 11 April 2016).
10. Alam Srinivas and T.R. Vivek. *IPL an Inside Story: Cricket and Commerce*. New Delhi: Roli Books, 2009, pp. 44–46.
11. Nalin Mehta, Jon Gemmel, and Dominic Malcolm. ' "Bombay Sport Exchange": Cricket, Globalisation, and the Future', *Sport in Society*, 12, no. 4/5 (May–June 2009), pp. 694–707.
12. Memon. *Wills Book of Excellence: One-Day Cricket*.
13. Srinivas and Vivek. *IPL an Inside Story: Cricket and Commerce*, p. 56.
14. David Rowe and Callum Gilmour. 'Global Sport: Where Wembley Way Meets Bollywood Boulevard', *Continuum: Journal of Media & Cultural Studies*, 23 no. 2 (April 2009), pp. 171–182.

15. Ajita Shashidhar. 'Each IPL Franchise Could Be Worth $5 Billion', *Outlook Business*, 8 March 2008. http://www.outlookbusiness.com/article_v3.aspx?artid= 100640 (accessed 30 March 2015).

16. Nitin Naik. 'Spider Camera Irks Players', *The Times of India*, 21 April 2011. https:// timesofindia.indiatimes.com/spider-camera-irks-players/articleshow/8042471. cms (accessed 19 June 2016).

17. Ivo Tennant. 'A Sport for the Fast Food generation', on *ESPNCricinfo*, 8 March 2011. http://www.espncricinfo.com/innovation/content/story/504671.html (accessed 21 March 2016).

18. Richard Giulianotti. 'Supporters, Followers, Fans, and Flâneurs: A Taxonomy of Spectator Identities in Football'. *Journal of Sport & Social Issues*, 26, no. 1 (February 2002), pp. 25–46.

19. Interview with Gideon Haigh, November 2014.

20. J.A. 'Why Cricket's World Cup Is Full of Meaningless Games', *The Economist*, 15 February 2015. http://www.economist.com/blogs/economist-explains/2015/02/ economist-explains-13 (accessed May 21 2015).

21. Chris Schilling and Philip A. Mellor. 'Re-conceptualizing Sport as a Sacred Phenomenon', *Sociology of Sport Journal*, 31, no. 3 (September 2014), pp. 349–376.

22. Amarnath Amarasingam. 'Nationalism, Cricket and the Religio-Politics of Sport', *The Huffington Post*, 5 April 2011. http://www.huffingtonpost.com/amarn ath-amarasingam/nationalism-cricket-and-t_b_844034.html?   (accessed   3 June 2015).

23. Gaurav Kanthwal. 'Why It Took KXIP So Long to Show Up at Their Home Ground', *The Tribune*, 27 April 2015. http://www.tribuneindia.com/news/sport/ why-it-took-kxip-so-long-to-show-up-at-their-home-ground/72895.html (accessed 3 June 2015).

24. Rowe and Gilmour. 'Global Sport: Where Wembley Way Meets Bollywood Boulevard'.

25. Srinivasan Ramani. 'Cricket, Excesses and Market Mania', *Economic and Political Weekly*, 43, no. 10 (8–14 March 2008) http://links.org.au/node/309 (accessed 18 December 2010).

26. International Cricket Council (@ICC). Tweet '@ECB_Cricket has the best of Day One of the Fifth Test, dismissing @BCCI for just 148 before finishing 62/ 0 #EngvInd'. 15 August 2014, 11:31 pm. https://twitter.com/icc/status/5003414 55710609409 (accessed 16 November 2015).

27. ESPNCricinfo Staff. 'The Cronje Chronicles', on *ESPNCricinfo*, 22 July 2013. http://www.espncricinfo.com/ci/content/story/654219.html   (accessed   17 September 2015).

28. 'ESPN to Telecast Premier League', *The Times of India*, 10 August 2001. http:// timesofindia.indiatimes.com/ESPN-to-telecast-Premier-League/articleshow/ 1964583945.cms (accessed 17 September 2015).

29. PTI. 'Bhajji "slaps" Sreesanth, Makes Him Cry', *The Times of India*, 26 April 2008. http://timesofindia.indiatimes.com/india/Bhajji-slaps-Sreesanth-makes-him-cry/articleshow/2983882.cms (accessed 20 May 2015).

30. 'IPL 2015: Virat Kohli Breaks Players' Protocol, Meets Anushka Sharma during Match against DD', *Zee News*, 18 May 2015. http://zeenews.india.com/sports/cricket/ipl/ipl-2015-virat-kohli-breaks-players-protocol-meets-anushka-sharma-during-match-against-dd_1597128.html (accessed 20 May 2015).

31. ESPNCricinfo Staff. 'Shah Rukh Khan Gets Five-Year Ban from Wankhede', on *ESPNCricinfo*, 18 May 2012. http://www.espncricinfo.com/indian-premier-league-2012/content/story/565312.html (accessed 20 May 2015).

Chapter 5

1. Interview with Gideon Haigh, November 2014.

2. Paul Virilio. *Speed and Politics*. Translated by Mark Polizzotti. New York: Semiotext (e), 1986, p. 94.

3. Patrick M. Bray. 'Aesthetics in the Shadow of No Towers: Reading Virilio in the Twenty-first Century', *Yale French Studies*, 114 (2008), pp. 4–17.

4. Paul Virilio. *Pure War*. Translated by Mark Polizzotti. New York: Semiotext(e), 1983.

5. Rebecca Carlson and Jonathan Corliss. 'Rubble Jumping: From Paul Virilio's Techno-Dromology to Video Games and Distributed Agency', *Culture, Theory and Critique*, 48, no. 2 (2007), pp. 161–174.

6. C.L.R. James. *Beyond a Boundary* (1963). London: Yellow Jersey Press, 2005, p. 283. (From an article James had written for *The Cricketer*. 22 June 1957.)

7. Ayaz Memon. *Wills Book of Excellence: One-Day Cricket*. Kolkata (Calcutta), West Bengal: Orient Longman, 1992, pp. 15–16.

8. Nalin Mehta, 'Batting for the Flag: Cricket, Television and Globalization in India', *Sport in Society*, 12, no. 4 (May–June 2009), pp. 579–599.

9. Zygmunt Bauman. *Consuming Life*. Cambridge, UK: Polity Press, 2007, pp. 82–87.

10. Tony Blackshaw. *Zygmunt Bauman*. New York: Routledge, 2007, pp. 29–31.

11. Bauman. *Consuming Life*, pp. 35–38.

12. Michael Miller quoted in George Ritzer. *Enchanting a Disenchanted World*. Thousand Oaks, California, USA: Pine Forge Press, 2012

13. Osman Samiuddin. 'Sold Out', on *ESPNCricinfo*, 13 June 2008. http://www.espncricinfo.com/magazine/content/story/354158.html (accessed 21 March 2016).

14. BBC. 'Brazil World Cup Beer Law Signed by President Rousseff'. 6 June 2012. http://www.bbc.com/news/world-latin-america-18348012 (accessed 15 November 2015).

15. Zygmunt Bauman. 'Consuming Life', *Journal of Consumer Culture*, 1, no. 1, 2001, pp. 9–29.

16. Statistics compiled from *ESPNCricinfo*. http://stats.espncricinfo.com/ci/engine/
    player/35320.html?class=1;spanmin1=22+Nov+2011;spanval1=span;template=
    results;type=batting;view=innings (accessed 5 November 2015).
17. Ratna Bhushan. 'Sachin Tendulkar Delaying Retirement for Fear of Losing Big
    Endorsements?', *The Economic Times*, 8 September 2012. http://articles.econom
    ictimes.indiatimes.com/2012-09-08/news/33696665_1_sachin-tendulkar-har
    ish-krishnamachar-amit-enterprises (accessed 5 November 2015).
18. Mukul Kesavan. 'A Farewell Left Too Late', on *ESPNCricinfo*, 14 October 2013.
    http://www.espncricinfo.com/magazine/content/story/679265.html (accessed 5
    November 2015).
19. Baidurjo Bhose. 'BCCI Rides Roughshod over ICC's Future Tour Plans: Board
    Snubs South Africa with Series Invite to West Indies', *Daily Mail*, 2 September
    2013. http://www.dailymail.co.uk/indiahome/indianews/article-2409373/BCCI-
    rides-roughshod-ICCs-future-tour-plans-Board-snubs-South-Africa-series-inv
    ite-West-Indies.html#ixzz3tSYw2RGo (accessed 05 November 2015).
20. Garth Wattley. 'Sidekicks' Chance to Steal the Show', on *ESPNCricinfo*, 27
    October 2013. http://www.espncricinfo.com/magazine/content/story/682687.
    html (accessed 5 November 2015).
21. Dilip D'Souza. *Final Test: Exit Sachin Tendulkar*. Random House India, 2014.
22. PR Newswire. 'KKR Won More Than Just the IPL Trophy This Year', 13 June 2014.
    http://www.prnewswire.co.in/news-releases/kkr-won-more-than-just-the-ipl-
    trophy-this-year-262980871.html (accessed 22 November 2015).
23. Ivo Tennant. 'A Sport for the Fast Food generation', on *ESPNCricinfo*, 8 March
    2011.   http://www.espncricinfo.com/innovation/content/story/504671.
    html?wrap (accessed 21 March 2011).
24. Samiuddin. 'Sold Out'.
25. Ashis Nandy. 'The Tao of Cricket', in *A Very Popular Exile*. New Delhi: Oxford
    University Press, 2007, pp. 38–41.
26. Milan Kundera. *Slowness*. UK: Faber and Faber, 1996, p. 4.
27. Interview conducted in Delhi, 2015.

Conclusion

1. C.L.R. James. *Beyond a Boundary* (1963). London: Yellow Jersey Press, 2005,
   Preface.
2. Ayaz Memon. *Wills Book of Excellence: One-Day Cricket*. Kolkata (Calcutta),
   West Bengal: Orient Longman, 1992, p. 21.
3. David Foster Wallace. 'Federer as Religious Experience', *The New York Times*, 20
   August 2006. http://www.nytimes.com/2006/08/20/sports/playmagazine/20fede
   rer.html?pagewanted=all (accessed 15 November 2015).

4. Steve Redhead. 'Those Absent from the Stadium Are Always Right: Accelerated Culture, Sport Media, and Theory at the Speed of Light', *Journal of Sport and Social Issues*, 31, no. 3 (August 2007), pp. 226–241.

5. SutJhally. 'Cultural Studies and the Sports/Media Complex', in L. A. Wenner (Ed.), *Media, Sports, and Society*. Newbury Park, California: Sage, 1989, pp. 70–93.

6. Owen Gibson. 'Cricket May Have Embraced Technology Too Quickly, Says Hawk-Eye founder', *The Guardian*, 8 August 2013. http://www.theguardian.com/sport/2013/aug/08/cricket-embraced-technology-hawkeye-founder (accessed 15 June 2015).

7. Amit Gupta. 'The Globalization of Cricket: The Rise of the Non-West', *International Journal of the History of Sport*, 21, no. 2 (March 2004), pp. 257–276.

8. Brett Hutchins and David Rowe. *Sport Beyond Television: The Internet, Digital Media and the Rise of Networked Media Sport*. New York: Routledge, 2012.

9. Garry Whannel. 'Television and the Transformation of Sport', *Annals of the American Academy of Political and Social Science*, Vol. 625, *The End of Television? Its Impact on the World (So Far)* (September 2009), pp. 205–218.

10. Richard Giulianotti. 'Supporters, Followers, Fans, and Flâneurs: A Taxonomy of Spectator Identities in Football', *Journal of Sport & Social Issues*, 26, no. 1 (February 2002), pp. 25–46.

11. Patrick M. Bray. 'Aesthetics in the Shadow of No Towers: Reading Virilio in the Twenty-first Century', *Yale French Studies*, 114 (2008), pp. 4–17.

12. Paul Virilio. *Speed and Politics*. Translated by Mark Polizzotti. New York: Semiotext (e), 1986, p. 94.

13. Rebecca Carlson and Jonathan Corliss. 'Rubble Jumping: From Paul Virilio's Techno-Dromology to Video Games and Distributed Agency', *Culture, Theory and Critique*, 48, no. 2 (2007), pp. 161–174.

14. Zygmunt Bauman. *Consuming Life*. Cambridge, UK: Polity Press, 2007, pp. 82–87.

15. Zygmunt Bauman. 'Consuming Life', *Journal of Consumer Culture*, 1, no. 1 (2001), pp. 9–29.

16. Ibid.

Index

For the benefit of digital users, indexed terms that span two pages (e.g., 52–53) may, on occasion, appear on only one of those pages.

Figures are indicated by *f* following the page number